Pentecost 2019

Kathy — May your next 50 years be as blessed as the last 50

Glimpses oGRACE

> ### Reflections of a Life in Christ

David Duggan

DAVID G. DUGGAN

WESTBOW
PRESS
A DIVISION OF THOMAS NELSON

WestBow Press books may be ordered through booksellers or by contacting:

WestBow Press
A Division of Thomas Nelson
1663 Liberty Drive
Bloomington, IN 47403
www.westbowpress.com
1 (866) 928-1240

Because of the dynamic nature of the Internet, any web addresses or links contained in this book may have changed since publication and may no longer be valid. The views expressed in this work are solely those of the author and do not necessarily reflect the views of the publisher, and the publisher hereby disclaims any responsibility for them.

Any people depicted in stock imagery provided by Thinkstock are models, and such images are being used for illustrative purposes only.
Certain stock imagery © Thinkstock.

ISBN: 978-1-4908-1179-6 (sc)
ISBN: 978-1-4908-1180-2 (hc)
ISBN: 978-1-4908-1178-9 (e)

Library of Congress Control Number: 2013918790

Printed in the United States of America.

WestBow Press rev. date: 12/19/2013

When I was in my early 40's, I began writing a regular column for the newspaper sent to Episcopalians in the Diocese of Chicago. In "Faithwalk," I tried to describe my struggles as a believing Christian set against my background as a lawyer, single parent, son of aging parents, and sinner. This venture in self-analysis continued a process of trying to square my life with God's call to a Christian begun many years earlier, but the writing was, I believe an insight into how God can and does work in all lives. (I almost wrote "all believers' lives." While I am not inclined to believe that Christ saves all regardless of their baptism, confession and communion, I accept that a divine, omnipotent force can do as He will. And I believe that God uses non-believers as a fulcrum to test our own belief.)

Fast forward 20 years, and the columns have collected dust, but on re-reading them, I think they stand the test of time. So, I have decided to publish them in a book, adding a bit of commentary to provide the context. They have been arranged, not in the order they were written, but rather according to topic, topics suggested by the biblical narrative by which the Creator of the Universe loved us so much that he sent his only Son to die for us. I hope you enjoy them.

Chicago, IL 2013

Table of Contents

HEIRSHIP

Introduction:

For better or worse, our ancestors give us that first glimpse of grace, an insight into the divine desire to create, sustain, reprove and ultimately love us. I was blessed by having parents who were deeply committed to each other and, as long as their children were under roof, to having them raised in a Christian household. Not that our faith was worn on our sleeves or touted to the exclusion of others: we were taught tolerance of and respect for all, but also the importance of sacrifice and perseverance. My parents and grandparents were rewarded with long life, and the privilege of seeing their children and grandchildren achieve some measure of temporal success: but even more a continuation of that faith which through their examples they tried to impart. Sadly, in my own life, I was not able to replicate their example of a life-long commitment; yet my son hasn't held that against me (or his mother). These essays try to show how we live in the mid-point of a tradition that began on a cross and ends in eternal life.

Living in the Meantime

My father just celebrated his 80th birthday. At the party in his honor, he recalled that when he turned 21 and became eligible to vote, he did not know if he would make it to his 22nd. Under orders from his Commander in Chief, he was prepared to sacrifice all for the cause of freedom in this world, never certain of his reward in the next. Grateful for having reached his ninth decade in good health and prosperity, he asked for a moment of silence for those who did not live to see that day.

Sixty years and half-a-dozen full-scale conflicts after my father's wartime pondering, we appear no closer to the goal of peace promised by the Prince of Peace. Some may find that discouraging, but in those years, world population has doubled, world-wide life-expectancy has increased 50 percent, and world hunger—as a percentage of those who go to bed hungry—has declined. More importantly, the Gospel is preached in places that had been at the ends of the earth. The Kingdom may not yet be at hand, but it is less far away.

Jesus was remarkably cryptic about the coming of the Kingdom. Wars and rumors of war, famine, pestilence, earthquakes. St. John writes about horsemen of the apocalypse, the seven-headed Beast and the final battle between the forces of good and evil. People will take these as literal pre-figurements of the "end times," and look to the events of 9/11 and their aftermath, but how is what we are going through now any different from that which has occurred during the past 20 centuries of conflict and waiting.

Early on in the history of the Church, followers of the Way questioned when God was going to reward them for their faithfulness. St. Paul did not mince words. "The Lord will come as a thief in the night," he wrote the Thessalonians. To those who offered a secular blessing of "peace and safety," he warned, "destruction will come on them suddenly, as labor pains on a pregnant woman, and they will not escape." In the meantime, we are to work with our hands, be self-controlled and encourage one another by putting on faith and love as a breastplate and the hope of salvation as a helmet. These are defensive armaments, and St. Paul surely thought that we ought better to be defended against the cares of this world than to be preoccupied with the life of the world to come.

The final conflict is no more likely to come in my lifetime than in my father's or my son's. But between life in Christ and death to sin we can see that God's purpose is working itself out: in the still small voice of a prophet who tells us that within the walls of the City of God are believers, and a successor and a widow who needs our help. When every widow is comforted and every orphan's tear is dried, then I will see the Kingdom of God fulfilled.

Commemorating Commitment

This past summer, my parents celebrated a milestone that few of my contemporaries are likely to see: their 50th wedding anniversary. It is not merely that the throw-away society has affected marriages or that an epicurean lifestyle shortens life expectancy or that the narcissistic culture has turned commitment into a word to be avoided. (I scarcely have room to talk). More significantly, I suspect, is that the Christian commitment my parents made to each other, the mutual sacrifice that mirrors Christ's union to His Church and God's love for His people, are seen as archaic or irrelevant.

Fortunately, my parents did not see things that way. I have no illusions that my parents' marriage was a sort of Ozzie and Harriet stage play. Nor did our household bear a likeness to *Father Knows Best*. Early on, my father was plucked from his profession to serve his country, and my mother gave up a fur coat so that her children could have music lessons and instruments. When he was in his early 40's my father returned to school so that his company could have his additional skills. My mother immersed herself in volunteer work, perhaps to compensate. Ever the optimist, my mother recounted that she had been told by the priest who had married them that if she thought that marriage is a 50-50 proposition, she had a 50-50 chance of failing. To her, failure was not an option.

But the family pictures taken through the 50 years don't lie. They show two strong yet supportive people who know that the whole is greater than the sum of the parts. I have taken some of those pictures, a skill I learned from my father, but they were taken with the eye I inherited from my mother: an eye for form and structure, symmetry and color.

My sisters and I commemorated my parents' anniversary with a party. There they were surrounded by the products of their steadfast love: their three children raised to responsible adulthood, six grandchildren striving to make their mark on the world, and more than 50 friends, many of whom had traveled some distance to attend, and others who had shared every step of the way along their 50 years' journey. And though that journey may be closer to the end than to the beginning, the memories of their friendships forged in a life together will undoubtedly sustain them in their years to come.

Our tradition teaches us that marriage is not only a sacrament, but a partnership in all virtue. Blessed by a loving God, my parents have been examples to their children and now their children's children. It would be sufficient, I suppose that the secular world would extol my parents for their accomplishment. But I think it better that they be remembered for having shown the truth that when two or three are gathered in God's name, God is in the midst of them. For 50 years, my parents have proved that.

The Passing of an Era

My last link to the turn of the century, my 93-year old grandmother, died a short while ago. Not only was she my last link to the days almost before the automobile and literally before the airplane, but she was also our family's link to the Anglican church, and more specifically the world-wide Anglican communion. For as is plain from her maiden name, Dunbar, she claimed some Scottish ancestry, and the first Episcopal bishops in this country were actually consecrated in Scotland, because there, the bishops did not have to take an oath of allegiance to the English monarch. I've always felt somewhat proud of that link: a descendant of Anglican-rite Scotsmen, who called their ordained clergy "ministers," observed morning prayer and worshiped from the 1928 Prayer Book.

I mention this because with my grandmother's passing, an era has also passed, an era in which the Church was triumphant, our ethic was Protestant, and our culture derived from the British Isles. I doubt that those days will ever return, and many of us sense a loss at the demise of the world as we have known it. But because my grandmother was a Christian, and Christians believe that God is ultimately in control, perhaps the demise of that era will herald the birth of a new era, more diverse and tolerant, but rooted in the traditions of a church that within a century spread from barely a dozen frightened believers to the outer limits of civilization.

My grandmother was a child of that tradition, one of six children growing up in western Pennsylvania, outside of Pittsburgh. She was an athlete when young, played the piano and had a marvelous voice I can remember hearing when we sang hymns together. A young bride, she bore our mother, Lois, named after the Biblical Timothy's own grandmother, when she was scarcely 21. She ultimately left the area of her birth, and settled in the Chicago suburbs. There, she introduced my mother to my father, newly home from the service. He was repairing the road outside my grandparents' home before returning to college, and asked for some water. Forty-eight years ago, my parents were married in an Episcopal service in a white-framed chapel in Wayne, IL.

After stops in New Jersey and New Hampshire, my grandmother retired to Florida. One of the family jokes was that she wanted her ashes scattered along the main shopping drag of the city where she lived. But her ashes were placed next to those of my grandfather in the ground outside the church where they worshiped, recalling the words that God spoke to Adam long ago, "Remember that you are dust, and unto dust shall you return." That church is patterned on the oldest Anglican church on this continent, in Williamsburg, VA.

My grandmother was a strong and vibrant woman who outlived all my other grandparents and most of her friends. There is a tendency on the death of a matriarch to say that her memory will live on in her progeny, that her legacy of six grandchildren and now six great grandchildren survive her. But what I wish to say is that, as a child of God, and as a disciple of the church, Grandmother has returned to her heavenly home, free of the pain that plagued her later years, embraced in the arms of the Son of God, who rose from the dead to heal all our pain and comfort all our afflictions.

A Mother's Understanding

Somehow, mothers seem to know everything that matters about their sons. I can't speak to what mothers know about their daughters, but from my limited perspective, it may not matter as much. Mothers and daughters are bound by a common thread that surpasses knowledge. The broken thread of gender that separates mothers from sons somehow contributes to their intuitive knowledge.

From the limited evidence, Mary had this intuitive knowledge of Jesus. Soon after His birth she learned that her Son would cause the thoughts of many hearts to be revealed, though a sword would pierce her own soul. The Bible tells of only two conversations between an adult Jesus and His mother, though they must have had others. The first was at Jesus' first miracle, turning water into wine at the wedding at Cana. The second was as Jesus was nailed to the cross. From these two snippets, one can conclude that their relationship was contentious: Jesus rebuking His mother, who had sought her Son's divine intervention, claiming that His time had not yet come; and Jesus telling Mary to behold Him on the cross, then telling the beloved disciple John to behold his mother.

I suspect that every son who has heard God's word sees in his mother traces of our Lord's own mother: the patience coupled with gentle goading; the careworn, yet the inner beauty and strength. And I suspect that every mother who has held an infant son sees in him a trace of the Son of God: the light of the world, the hope for peace.

I thought of the depth of the mother-son relationship when seeing my own mother recently. Though separated by only 30 miles, we don't get together much. She has her life and I have mine, but we talked about how 25 years ago, I had graduated from college. It was one of the last times that my entire family of parents and sisters, grandmothers and grandfathers assembled. Though outwardly a time for celebration, that is not quite how I remembered it. It may strike some as curious that my college years were not the best of my life. I was young, far from home, an indifferent student, more interested in having fun to excess than in learning anything that would matter later. All that separated me from the Prodigal was that my father had two daughters to educate so he could not give me half.

But my mother, who had seen how I had worked before college, and knew something of my life since, had a different insight. She said that she doubted that I would have had the incentive to achieve what I had, had I not spent those years in wastrel pursuits. To her it was important that I had come home. I would never have guessed that, but her intuitive understanding of the secrets of my heart gave me a glimpse of the divine love we all seek.

A Father's Son

For the past year, I played a role for which I am marvelously ill-suited: that of a single parent to my teenage son. Ill-suited, not only because I've had little experience and less training, but also because I have neither patience with nor interest in the popular culture. My tastes and attitudes firmly placed in the 18th century, I can't imagine what people find interesting about modern music, body adornment and philosophy.

Yet my son's presence under my roof has offered a degree of connection to the world that I have otherwise lacked. Concerns over school quality and insurance rates, teenage violence and adult duplicity have taken on something other than academic import. For at least this reason, his return to spend the rest of adolescence with his mother has left me with a feeling of emptiness and disconnection.

Judging from the Bible, the father-son relationship is the most enigmatic around. The dashed paternal expectations and the filial scheming; the shared desire to make the other proud coupled with studied indifference to each other; and the impulse to eclipse one's forbears are all part of the patterns described in the history of God's people. From Abraham, Isaac, Jacob and Joseph, through David, Absalom and Solomon, to Jesus, the Bible's accounts of the father-son relationship give a rich chronicle of behavioral excess. Some might even say that the most poetic and prophetic words in the Old Testament are found in David's lament over the death of his rebellious son Absalom: "would God that I had died for thee." And this is not to mention the lessons Jesus drew to illustrate His own life as Son, and ours as God's children. The Prodigal, the landlord's emissary who is killed so that the tenants can inherit the vineyard, and the bridegroom to whose wedding the king invites all with a garment yet throws the one guest without one into the darkness, all point to a Father who loves us dearly, but struggles to find the words to say so.

My woman friends sometimes find this emphasis on the male half of humanity to be an indictment of our tradition. They think that by ignoring a woman's experience as mother and daughter, sister and wife, the Bible puts too much emphasis on destruction and death, vengeance and military victory. Of course, the Bible also tells of healing and reconciliation, comfort and sacrifice, virtues that are genderless. But as the only son of an only son, with an only son, yet with a mother and two sisters who easily burst my bubble, I can only say that the y-chromosomes of the genetic code conclusively prove how helpless we are without God's love and mercy, justice and forgiveness.

My son may not yet appreciate the value of his roots which stem back even further than the 18th century. But as he finds his own way through the thicket of life, I pray that his journey will end in eternal life in God's Son.

A Father's Role in His Child's Faith

When my eight-year-old son came to visit me during last year's Holy Week, I had a revelation of sorts: fathers have at least as important a role in their children's moral and religious development as do mothers. Although this revelation may place me somewhere between a master of the obvious and a male chauvinist, I dare say that many children liken their heavenly Father to the earthbound variety. This stems not only from the language in which Jesus taught us to pray, but also, I suspect, from some of their common characteristics: fathers are likely to be more distant (or at least perceived to be so), they are prone to work six days a week (unlike mothers who work seven) and when they lay down the law they have the means to enforce it.

But with the advent of dual-income families and the rise of single-parent households—most headed by mothers—a child's perception of God may be skewed. The difficulty of communicating with a distant God may be equated with the difficulty of communicating with an absent parent. The unconditionality of God's love for all his children may be impossible to convey to a child who experiences, if at all, a parent's love on weekends or alternate holidays. Non-custodial fathers, of whom I am one, therefore have a particular responsibility to assure that their children grow to the full measure of the stature of Christ.

Paradoxically, the single, non-custodial parent's duty to raise his children in God's fear and favor creates an opportunity to assure them of God's love even if their parents could not love each other. Though children of divorce may pray for a reunion of their parents and a return to a "normal" family life, the non-custodial parent, by integrating worship and prayer into the time he spends with his children, can help their prayers be more than pipe dreams.

That is why I took the time to involve my son in Holy Week services. Even though he attends church regularly with his mother, and undoubtedly prefers "quality time" spent throwing a ball to any time spent talking to God, the trade-off is a poor one in the end. My son may not see church as the vehicle to adulthood as I did, learning big words and grown-up rituals, but he should see his dad down on his knees, begging God's forgiveness.

I may not be able to lead my son into an understanding of the Christian faith, but I hope that he has learned that his father needs to seek God's forgiveness as much as he does. And if he has learned that, then he will have learned the foundation of a faith in a heavenly Father who loves him as no human father can.

[Author's note: This was one of my earliest essays, and while it sounds dated (references to "quality time" and "pipe dreams"), the message that a parent owes his children an obligation to raise them in the faith, and that the best way to do that is for the parent to seek God's forgiveness remains true. The upshot is that, more than 20 years after this was written, my son is a committed Christian.]

Postscript to Heirship:

Both of my parents have gone to their eternal reward, achieving the Biblical span of four-score years given those of strength. I spoke at their several memorial services (occasioned by schedules and their living at a retirement facility where not everyone can get around) and somehow kept it together through all of them until the Marine Corps honor guard presented me with the flag draping my father's

VOCATION

Introduction:

For most of my adult life I earned my daily bread as a lawyer—initially in the employ of others and for nearly 20 years, as a solo practitioner. My practice was varied, but a good portion of it was defending those accused of federal crimes. I never got rich doing it, and nearly lost my license because of advice I gave a client. But if a person and a secular vocation could ever be perfectly matched, I dare say it was lawyering and me. Argumentative to a fault, nit-picking and bent on logical exposition with a highly competitive streak, I took to the law as a duck to water. Of course, Jesus reserved some of his most caustic criticisms for lawyers, and for many years I struggled with this: was this just a game which I was good at? Given the almost fore-ordained outcome of the criminal trials, was I playing a role in an orchestrated kabuki dance? Or was there something to it? These essays confront that dilemma, providing some explanation into the process by which our nation was conceived in liberty, dedicated to the proposition that all are created equal and treated as such before the law, and sustained by "the spirit [which] remembers that not even a sparrow falls to earth unheeded; the spirit of Him who, near two thousand years ago, taught mankind that lesson it has never learned, but has never quite forgotten—that there may be a kingdom where the least shall be heard and considered side-by-side with the greatest," in the immortal words of Judge Learned Hand.

Toiling in the Vineyards of the Law

A while back one of my favorite law professors died. Though I would not have guessed it at the time, more than anyone else, he inspired me to pursue the particular path in the law that I have taken. More importantly, however, this man inspired an entire generation of lawyers who became governor and judge, prosecutor and public defender. I would not be stretching the truth to say that this man's contributions to legal scholarship were the most significant of the last half-century.

For a long time, however, this professor toiled in an academic wilderness, his ideas out of fashion, his scholarship scorned, even by our nation's highest court. It was a tribute to his longevity, as well as his patience, persistence and gentlemanly grace that toward the end of his life his ideas became accepted, perhaps even mainstream. In a sense, he fulfilled the promise of his life—that in legal process might be found a place where the guilty would be fairly punished and the unjustly accused would be set free.

Before they knew him as Lord and Savior, Jesus' disciples knew Him as Rabbi, teacher. Not just any teacher, but one who taught with authority, and not just any authority, but with the authority of the Father. The depth of His teachings has pre-occupied theologians and scholars for two millennia, and I can scarcely add anything to the volume of discourses and meditations on Our Lord, not as moral example, divine healer, or Prince of Peace, but as friend and teacher.

This much I do know. Christ's teachings, radical as they were for the time, and even by His disciples little understood, were ignored during His life on earth. Even now, they are honored more in the breach than in the observance. Consider how little of the earth the meek have inherited, or how we still worry about the morrow and condemn those caught in adultery, or how few of the talents we have been given we will bring back to the Master when it comes time to settle our accounts.

Christ taught that He came not to change the law, but to fulfill it. The authorities in the law mocked this message and killed the messenger. But twenty centuries after Christ came into the world to enlighten sinners like me, His teaching that He is the Way, the Truth and the Life is a lesson that the world has not quite learned, but has never quite forgotten. And Jesus' pointing to a Kingdom where the least is counted with the greatest, and where He welcomes the lowest criminal into Paradise on his day of reckoning, is the lesson I have followed as I toil in the vineyards of the law.

The God of Covenant

A couple of months ago, I was feeling particularly anxious about my life: clients who wouldn't listen, opponents who couldn't understand, and briefs that weren't writing themselves. Seeking spiritual counsel in that wilderness of noise, one dreary Saturday I went to hear a Franciscan friar speaking at my parish.

As is my habit (pun intended), I arrived late, and found a place where I had a clear view of the Franciscan, but hopefully, he could not notice my entrance. Just at that moment, the Franciscan contrasted the God of contract with the God of covenant; the God of Saul of Tarsus with the God of the Apostle Paul; the God who holds us to our bargain with the God who always welcomes us back in forgiveness. How ironic for a lawyer.

I confess that I have an easier time believing in Saul's God of a bargained contract. So elegantly simple, so determinate and precise. The God who loves me, even in my radical brokenness as the Franciscan put it, can't really know the whole story.

But shortly after that, I read of the conversion of a convicted murderer; how after a life of addiction and aimlessness, he had found God's love in an 8-by-12 foot cell, locked away from society behind a veil of razor wire. I represent people like him, but am always cautious about sharing my faith that the same God who loves them inside their physical prison also loves me inside my spiritual cell. They come to me for legal advice, not moral guidance.

This converted convict wrote how the spiritual leaders of the 21st century were being prepared in our nation's penal institutions. Hard as that may be to believe, those of whom much has been forgiven can powerfully witness to the power of God's love. Prisoners truly know how God has taken the broken and made it whole, and I believed that man who had been freely given a new life in Christ. How ironic that a lawyer would be ministered to by one of those whom he serves.

His Trial, Our Triumph

As a trial lawyer, I am continually fascinated by the four separate accounts of Jesus' trial before Herod and Pilate, the Sanhedrin and ultimately the people of Jerusalem. The back and forth between tribunals and potentates, the symbolic washing of hands and rending of garments, and Jesus' silence in the face of accusations all have their parallels in modern criminal procedure. Scholars spend their lives interpreting the differences in the Gospels, trying to decide what Jesus said and what he didn't, why Pilate and Herod were enemies before the trial, but became friends afterwards, or how could Matthew have known what Pilate's wife had dreamed.

I can't add anything to these debates, which seem rather beside the point anyway. As anyone who has ever tried a case before will tell you, it is hard to get two witnesses to agree on small points, but merely because they disagree about the color of the defendant's clothes doesn't mean that he was not wearing them. "The devil is in the details" rings true even in the Bible.

But what fascinates me more than anything else is how the world has changed since that trial long ago. Even in my bailiwick, known for the snail's pace of its development, we do not try and convict, sentence and execute those accused of crimes all in one day. Though the printing press first printed the Bible, it later published the law so that all could learn God's way of justice and truth.

Philosophers may chalk up the changes across two millennia to the random succession of independent events. Cynics say that those who see an external force afoot may as well believe in UFOs, and besides, what's wrong with the summary execution of a hardened criminal? But Christians see the hand of a loving God who against all reason condemned His Only Son to death.

Like those whom I represent in modern courtrooms far away from the public spectacle in a Jerusalem courtyard, Jesus faced a heavy sentence from rulers anxious to protect their authority. But because He bore even my sins, they too are assured of eternal life.

The Tenant of Our Hearts

Both my father and I have spent a large chunk of our adult lives as landlords. When I was younger my father often called on me to help him out by resolving tenant complaints, collecting rents, making sure the apartments were painted and clean. Though maybe I should have known better when I became a householder, as I have been suffering through the worst real estate market in 25 years, the advantages of owning property rented out to others still outweigh the disadvantages. I am also glad that I can do my bit to improve the little corner of creation that God has entrusted to me, perhaps even the lives of my tenants.

Jesus often used examples from the landlord–tenant relationship to describe our relationship to God: the landlord who gave each of his overseers talents before traveling to a distant land, who on his return to find out who had invested those talents, threw the wicked and slothful servant into the abyss. The crafty manager who cut a number of his landlord's bills to get immediate payment, yet still earned his overseer's favor. Even the parable of the prodigal son, who would have preferred being one of his father's hired servants to slopping pigs in a far country, is filled with the images of landowning. Together, they point to the God of Judgment who still bestows his mercy on us though we scarcely deserve it.

The parable that has always troubled me, however, presents the landlord who kept sending messengers to his tenants to collect the portion of the crops due him. The messengers returned beaten and bloodied, so the landlord finally sent his son on the theory that the tenants would listen to him. Relying on a legal system we moderns would find beyond bizarre, the tenants killed the son so they could inherit the vineyard. In an odd twist, Jesus did not finish the story. He asked his listeners, who included a number of priests and Pharisees, what should happen to the tenants. They gave the obvious answer: that the tenants should meet a wretched end.

Thankfully the fate of the landlord's messengers never befell me, and I have been able to collect my own rents in hopes of keeping Caesar and God at bay. Though Jesus reminded his listeners that 1,000 years before him, the psalmist wrote how the stone which the builders rejected had become the capstone of the Lord's arch over us all, it took Jesus' death and resurrection for the religious leaders to realize what they had done. But as an heir living under that arch of protection, I have been freed to devote some portion of my life to the cultivation of God's creation.

Never having a place he could call home, Jesus was buried in a borrowed tomb, the ultimate tenant on this earth. Yet God has shown his mercy on us, not by visiting us with the death we so richly deserve, but with new life in the ultimate tenant of our hearts, His Son.

The Ultimate Prize

Last fall, I attended two sporting events (okay, one was pay-per-view) where a Biblical citation was prominently displayed. Each time, my companion asked me what that chapter and verse said, and each time, I'm embarrassed to say, I pled ignorance. Perhaps ironically, each time, the so-called good guys in these contests won.

Like many, I suspect, I find these and other public displays of religious belief troubling. An athlete who attributes his victory to Jesus Christ and Divine Will comes close to saying that his opponent was not blessed or that his own defeats were the work of the devil. Can this be true of a God who promises to be with us always, who has numbered the hairs on our head, and who does not let a sparrow fall to the ground without knowing about it?

As a one-time athlete who struggled back when with a search for physical excellence (and continues to do so despite the advancing effects of middle age), I have questioned whether a divine hand lies behind my athletic success and failures. The best answer that I can come up with is that I have learned more of life and meaning and myself in defeat than I have in victory. That answers those in the popular culture who claim that those who thank Jesus for their triumphs are kooks, for the Christian message is that God turns defeat into victory.

From chains in a Roman prison, St. Paul often drew on athletic metaphors in his letters back to the Greek churches that he had visited. Perhaps this was in keeping with the Hellenic culture which Paul, as a Hellenized Jew of the Diaspora, knew intimately. The

Greeks, more than others, extolled the physical ideal for its own sake. But the metaphors, drawn from the contests of the ancient Olympics, would have died out unless they had universal application to the lives of all who search for the hand of a loving God behind their daily strivings.

Paul, who counted all as lost for the surpassing love of Christ, wrote that he had run the race, fought the good fight, pressing on to the goal to win the prize for which God had called him heavenward. Our striving to win the ultimate fight, over sin and death, is more important than any victory over any mortal opponent.

Turning the Other Cheek

Earlier this year, I received a real lesson in turning the other cheek. I was representing a defendant in one of the gang conspiracy trials you read and hear about in the popular media. It wasn't enough to be defending my client against the charges brought by the Government, task enough to be sure, but I also had to defend myself against one of the other defense lawyers who for some reason had come to hate me and made no secret of that.

Those who know me best claim that patience is not my long suit, and I confess to having flown off the handle at the slightest provocation on more than one occasion in the past. But even I was put off by the vitriol of the comments. Rather than join this fellow lawyer in the race to the gutter, however, I resisted the temptation, remembering how foolish and even remorseful I had felt when I have engaged in similar conduct.

For some reason, this passivity was not completely satisfactory, either. Sticking up for myself would have felt much better. And I confess to a degree of moral smugness in claiming the high ground.

But this experience in self-restraint reminded me how Jesus told his followers that they would be persecuted and vilified for following Him, for taking up their own crosses, for forgiving and praying for those who hate them. Was I doing anything less than what my faith demands of me?

In the riveting movie, *Dead Man Walking*, a convicted double murderer tried to make peace with the parents of his victims by finally accepting responsibility for his actions. His appeals for clemency having run out, he saw clearly that his denial of his guilt had been for nought. Strapped to his deathbed, the tubes that would carry the lethal cocktail already inserted in his veins, he told those parents that he wanted his death to atone for the lives he had taken. The peace that had eluded his violent life came moments later. And I remembered how Jesus prayed for those who tortured him before committing his spirit into the hands of His Father.

Postscript to Vocation:

I spent the last years of my parents' lives involved in legal disputes over fraudulent investments (nobody should have to experience that, least of all in their later years). When these were resolved on fairly good terms, I started looking forward to a less hectic life. Then I was hit by a runaway car driven, if that's the word and if you can believe it, by a personal injury lawyer who had fainted at the wheel. After he was exonerated in traffic court (this was C[r]ook County, Illinois, home of the judicial fix), I decided that I could not in good conscience continue to be involved in the profession: I no longer believed in it. The recent revelations about tortured confessions and wrongful convictions have confirmed my beliefs. Some three years ago, I shut down my practice and have retired to a life of reflection and more recently, community activism (I guess I am still infected with that bug). I haven't yet written my novel. Oh, and that lawyer who vexed me many years ago? He recently killed himself. May he rest in a peace that so far as I could tell, he never knew in this life.

CREATION

Intro to Creation:

I have no doubt that we live in a created order, and have no interest in debating evolution or natural selection or fossils or aliens who have interbred with us. Still, my intellectual curiosity tells me that I should at least pay attention to these strains of thought, which are reprised in many more mundane inquiries: Do we have free will or are we chessmen playing out a divine game? How can we know that Jesus lived, let alone died for us? These essays try to put these inquiries into the context of faith which asks not so much why the world exists and in its physical integrity is so screwed up, but what is the alternative to belief, and where does that get you?

The Light that Shines Through the Darkness

For the last six summers, my extended family has spent a week together on the Western Shore of Lake Michigan. Because the place is a state secret, I can't disclose its location, but its solitude, the presence of all who are dear to me, and the majesty of the lake and the shoreline dunes stir reflection on the meaning of life.

A high point of each day there is the sunset. One of the few drawbacks to living in Chicago is that we don't see the sun set over water. But I have been blessed to see them in Florida, California and Hawaii, so I really have nothing to complain about. A sunset over water is one of God's little gifts to us, reminding us that He is the author of all beauty and glory in our lives.

This past trip a few of us were treated to a spectacular sunset. Though the sun had dipped behind two ridges of purple clouds, their edges were lined in gold. Between these edges a silver dagger of light spread to reveal a pale robin's egg blue, a reminder of the coming day. At the horizon, glowing embers of red looked like coals in a hearth, and in the distance, a cloud formation loomed up from the lake like the mountains from Yosemite Valley. Overhead a lone gull was silhouetted against the darkening sky.

God has spent a great deal of time speaking to us through sky and water. The rainbow after the flood that spared Noah; the healing of the Syrian general Namaan; Elijah's ascension in the chariot of fire; Jesus' baptism in the Jordan, greeted by the dove and heralded by the voice announcing that He was God's beloved Son and that we should listen to Him.

Though scientists tell us that water is whence we all come, Jesus tells us that Heaven is where we who believe in Him are to return. The light that shone through the darkness of that sunset over Lake Michigan showed me the truth of His promise.

Toiling in the Garden

Some 30 years ago, to earn spending money for college, I cut my neighbors' lawns and tended to their gardens. This was not a labor that came naturally (my mother once remarked that the only time she had a green thumb was when she spray painted some bushes that had died over the winter), and I vowed that when I grew up, I would have someone else do this work for me.

Like many an adolescent vow, I've found this one hard to keep. Although it is a stretch to say that I enjoy gardening, I derive a sense of satisfaction from digging in the soil, planting flowers and watching them grow. And my neighbors' compliments almost compensate for the aches that beset my post-adolescent body.

I thought about these mixed feelings that my gardening inspires as I pulled weeds from a new wildflower bed I built and planted this year. Because I did not study botany or horticulture in college, I was never certain whether that which I uprooted was a weed or the beginnings of a flower.

My limitations as a gardener came home to me as I listened to the familiar parable about the seed sewn on rocky soil. This is one of Jesus' few parables that comes with its own interpretation, but Jesus frequently taught his followers with metaphors drawn from man's first encounter with God in a garden. The wheat and the tares that must be reaped together, then separated because their roots had become entwined. The laborers in the vineyard who each derive the same reward no matter how long they had toiled. The tiny mustard seed that becomes the greatest plant. Together, they point to the God who not only has created us in His image from the soil, but who has nurtured us with His Word and sacraments, and who will harvest us to eternal life through His Son.

But unlike the plants sprouting in my garden, God knows by name each of those in whose heart He has planted His Spirit. Though no plant in my garden enjoys that comfort, it is one for which I am thankful.

The Word Made Flesh

For a long time, I have resisted going on-line, using the Internet in this dot-com crazy world. It is not that I am opposed to technological innovation (I use the telephone and even own a computer on which I compose these essays), but I prefer real letters signed by real people put in real envelopes bearing real postage to messages sent over common lines in some mythical location called "cyberspace." The connection I feel to the author more than makes up for the delay in receiving the message.

The tools of modern communication may herald a new age of Christendom, as web sites replace televangelists who replaced tent preachers. Jesus himself preached to thousands, we are told, and I have been moved to tears when assembled in large gatherings of believers. But Jesus never wrote a book, and indeed the only evidence of his being able to write at all was inscribed in sand, listing the sins of the accusers of the woman taken in adultery, where the words could be easily erased. How ironic that the Internet generation uses the sands of time, mutated into semi-conductors, to transmit its own deletable messages.

St. Paul had no illusions about the dangers of imperfect communication. Time and again in his Epistles, he writes how word had reached him that one of the communities of Christians which he had come to know and love had strayed from the true teachings. Thankfully for us, rather than rely on a Mediterranean gossip tree to reply to what he had heard, he wrote down his instructions and admonitions, his reasons and his own faith-based experiences.

An omnipotent God could have sent his Son to any age. That he chose an age of oral tradition, little supported with the written Word, shows His concern with how we process messages. As I have learned and felt in my life 20 centuries from the events most recently recorded in the Bible, the testimony of a live witness is more compelling to his listeners than any written word. But in order that others may understand and believe, the written word takes on the measure of the author.

At Christmas, we hear that in the beginning was the Word, that the Word was God, and that the Word became flesh. In our breakneck race for the blessings of impersonal cyberspace, I am blessed by the One who came through time and space, to share a few Words with us, but more importantly, to share His life, that we who hear and share His Word might have life more abundantly.

[Author's Note: Obviously I could not continue in my latter-day Luddite-ism, and shortly after this article was published I succumbed to the pressures of the age and went on-line. I similarly resisted joining facebook or other social networks until well after most people I know. Still, the point remains: how can we build the connections of a community if our only points of tangency occur over the Internet? How can God use the blessings of our technology to make His purpose known? The only answer I can come up with is in God's time, we will find out.]

The Building in Our Hearts

For the last several months, I've been treated to a ballet of construction workers outside my window tying the steel together on the latest Loop skyscraper. With uncanny grace and precision, this hard-hatted team tightrope walk eight-inch-wide beams, scale steel columns using only their hands and feet, and straddle 50 foot girders suspended in the air to jockey them into place—all without a safety net or tether. Though I'm a weekend warrior around the house, with a few scars to show for it, this awe-inspiring display is a welcome distraction from peering into the computer screen. Exciting as this spectacle is though, I confess that I miss the narrow sliver of Lake Michigan that I could see before construction reached the level of my floor.

Much of the Bible centers around building: Noah's ark, the Tower of Babel, Solomon's Temple, the Temple built after Cyrus let the Israelites return from Babylon, the cubits and spans, lavers and hewers. Though we can scarcely comprehend in our modern science of construction these sizes and shapes, skills and tasks, all bear witness to a race of master builders. Even secular history has come to believe that the pyramids were built by the Hebrews while in slavery to Pharaoh. No wonder he didn't want them to leave. By devoting much of their sacred literature to their physical building of God's kingdom, the Israelites showed their devotion to the Master Builder who set the line on the foundations of the earth.

Jesus also used parables and metaphors from the world of building to describe the Kingdom. The man who built his house on stone, and not sand to withstand the flood; the man who tore down his barns and built bigger ones only to have his life claimed that night; the many mansions in His Father's house. They point to the God who not only laid the cornerstone of our physical world, but who is more infinitely concerned that we build within our hearts the love of all those whom He has created in His image.

The son of a carpenter, Jesus knew well the dangers of building to house His Kingdom. While foxes dug their holes and birds crafted their nests, Jesus had no place to lay His head. And when Peter—the rock on whom Jesus built His Church—wanted to build booths on the Mount of Transfiguration for Elijah, Moses and the resplendent Christ, Jesus instead went into the crowd to cure the paralytic boy.

The building outside my window stands as a monument to the willingness of others to dare great things that all may prosper. But the building in our hearts of a place where Christ reigns stands as the true measure of our faith. For this faith reaches beyond the walls to touch all who yearn for a place where Christ is known.

Postscript to Creation:

One of my brothers in faith and near life-long friend is a renowned pathologist who volunteers his time both to help exonerate the wrongfully convicted and to sit ring-side at boxing matches. As devoted a scientist as I have known, he has embraced the Gospel message of a Savior who rose from the dead. People can of course whip themselves into a frenzy over just about anything, so my friend's belief, contrary to medical science as we know it, proves absolutely nothing. What it shows though is that in our quest for certainty we will never be satisfied; yet if we accept that faith in the Lord is the beginning of wisdom, the doors answering all questions will be opened unto us.

SELF-OFFERING

Introduction:

Like many, I suspect, I spend a good part of my life wondering, "what if . . ." What if I had gone to a different college or not gone to law school, or taken this job or that? Pointless as this exercise may be, at least it gives me a perspective of counting the blessings of the paths I have taken. And it shows that the only meaning that our lives have is what they give to others, not in the bargained-for exchange of money for education or services or things, but in the implicit trades of our time for that which cannot be valued: friendship, wisdom, connections, even love. These essays try to put that concept of self-offering, which Jesus exemplified in his "one oblation of himself once offered," into the ongoing pageant of my life.

The Blood of Redemption

Thanks to good genes and a G-rated lifestyle (or so says a pathologist friend of mine), I have a rare blood type. So every 8 weeks or so (barring a cold or laziness), I dutifully trundle off to the local hospital to donate a pint, enduring in the process needle sticks and questions too personal to be repeated in polite company. Thanks again to a steady diet of rare cheeseburgers, my iron level climbs back up in a hurry, and I feel no after-effects.

I have often wondered who have been the beneficiaries of my gifts. Hemophiliacs and cancer survivors, perhaps, AIDS patients and accident victims probably. Too squeamish ever to have become a doctor, I am gratified that in this small way I can attend to the medical needs of others less fortunate. And this way, I can defend my dietary preference against those who claim that no animal should die that I may enjoy a meal.

Shedding blood as an act of atonement has ancient and powerful symbolism. At the time of Christ, the Kidron River behind the great Temple ran red with the blood of animals slain to atone for the sins of the faithful. God's original covenant with Abraham was sealed between the halves of animals cleaved to show that He, taking the form of a flaming torch, had united Himself for all time to us. Of course, Christ's blood, shed from Temple courtyard to Golgotha cross for our redemption, is the ultimate symbol of God's holy mystery, tying us as if by spiritual umbilical cord to Christ's death. Thankfully for us who would never do ill to an animal, let alone offer one as a substitute for our own redemption, Christ's Last Supper joins the symbolism of sacrifice to our need for a communal offering.

My blood will never be for those who receive it the gift of life eternal. For that, they must look to the Divine Healer. But I am grateful that in my own small way, I can offer a bit of myself in remembrance of Him whose blood was shed for me.

The Terror of Our Belief

I went to law school with a man who took some of the shotgun pellets that felled Jonathan Myrick Daniels. A seminarian at Episcopal Divinity School killed in Alabama in the civil rights struggles of 1965, Daniels is commemorated by the church on August 14. My law school classmate, a former Roman Catholic priest, spent much of his 20s recovering from his wounds. Whether it is the comparatively complacent life of a lawyer, or the fact that he married a cousin of New York Yankee centerfielder Bernie Williams and fathered five children, he is now the picture of health and looks 10 years younger than his 60+ years.

Few of us will ever have to confront the terror of our belief in justice, righteousness and peace the way my classmate did. Even fewer will pay the price with no hope for redemption this side of the grave. But it cannot be martyrdom that motivates these saints, that drives them to sacrifice for a Savior who endured all they have and worse. Martyrdom leads too quickly to self righteousness and its evil twin—a disdain for us lesser mortals who choose compromise and conciliation, perhaps even cowardice over the barricades.

I have no idea what motivated Jonathan Daniels or my classmate. Certainly the cause of freedom for those whose yoke of slavery had not been lifted for 100 years. Perhaps the spirit of the age which pitted young against old, rich against poor, hawk against dove, black against white. Maybe even the fear of being left behind in the cultural shift, of being afraid to be a pacifist in the battle for the nation's soul.

Jesus confronted our tendency to shirk our duty to Him. Those who loved their lives, their father and mother more than Him, were not worthy of the Kingdom. But who can live up to this? Better yet, who can die to it?

St. Paul endured all to know the surpassing love of Christ and counted all as lost that he might be found in Him. The original survivor, three times Paul sailed around the Mediterranean, preaching the gospel with no thought for himself, withstanding shipwrecks and stocks, five floggings, three canings and a stoning. Before he was beheaded, not as a Roman citizen as was his birthright, but as a rebel outside the city's walls, he wrote from prison that in these afflictions, we are more than conquerors, for neither death nor life, neither the present nor the future, neither angels nor demons, nor anything can separate us from the love of God that is in Christ Jesus.

The God Who Transcends
Time and Culture

People who know me only from my church involvement find it hard to believe that I once sang in the same boys' choir with Robin Williams. Though our paths have taken remarkably different turns since the sixth grade, I wonder whether his dramatic gift for comedy and voice impressions may have been kindled during after-school rehearsals in the choir loft of the suburban parish where we lived.

I thought about that recently as I returned to that suburban parish for a Hallmark holiday celebration with my parents. I don't go back there much anymore. The parish is a lot different now, and I know very few people. Many of my parents' friends have died, or left the area, or fallen away, and next to none of my contemporaries have stayed with the church where they were raised.

Of course, the world is a lot different now than it was in the early '60s when Robin and I sang communion hymns at the 9:15 service. I have many more life experiences against which to measure the words inviting us all to partake in the body and blood of the Son of God, whose last supper calls us into fellowship with our heavenly Father. But as the only one of my parents' three children who has stayed with the church of our upbringing, I wondered whether the church has been more concerned with the voice impressions than the message behind them. Hard as it may be to believe, the Episcopal church—which gave this country not only its first religious hospital, but also its first African-American ordained clergyman—has been both relevant and multicultural since its inception.

The Acts of the Apostles tells how Paul struggled with the multiculturalists of his day. In the Athenian agora, amidst the altars to the gods we studied in sixth grade mythology, stood an altar inscribed to an unknown god. Paul told the assembly of pantheists that the God unknown to them was the God closest to them, the God in whom we all live and move and have our being.

Refusing to be bound by the Athenians' notions of a god carved in the ornament of the day, Paul's God of human history has spanned not only the varieties of human cultures, but also the limitations of human time. But Paul's message ringing true across the boundaries of time and space is that this God requires people everywhere to repent, because He has fixed a day on which He will have the world judged in righteousness by his Son whom He has appointed and whom He raised from the dead.

Answering the Call to Die

The older sister of friend I have known for 35 years died a short while ago. In the mid-1970s when I was in law school, and she was beautiful beyond words, we had been social companions. But we had lost touch with each other, except through her brother. From him I learned that her adult life had been one of pain and demons that no one could exorcise, perhaps the consequence of life in a lane that I could not keep up with. Powerless (or perhaps unwilling) to reach out to her during her lifetime, I kept a long-standing professional commitment rather than go to her funeral.

In one of Jesus' harshest statements, he told one would-be follower who needed first to bury his father: "Let the dead bury the dead." Some comfort in the face of my dilemma, I suppose. Besides, Jesus' statement could always be interpreted figuratively (insert "spiritually dead") as following it literally would soon present a public health crisis.

Jesus' statement and the death of my friend's sister called to mind Dietrich Bonhoeffer's remark that when God calls a man (or woman), He calls him to die. For Bonhoeffer, the German-born but American-trained theologian, this remark was both a literal and figurative prophecy. Active in the German dissenter church during World War II, and a plotter against Hitler, he was killed on the Fuhrer's direct orders in a Nazi prison camp just days before the Allies freed it.

Though Bonhoeffer's sacrificial life and death bore little resemblance to that of my friend's sister, each received the same reward—strife closed in the sod. For those of us who do not daily face the life and death consequences of our actions, however, answering the call to die paradoxically frees us from our earthly concerns over earning a living, educating our children and planning for retirement.

Hearing Christ's promise of eternal life in Him comes too late for many. The day of the funeral of a woman who died far too young, I prayed that she heard God's call before she breathed her last.

Confessing the Faith in Christ Crucified

The brutal murder of my fellow lawyer, Episcopalian and former resident of Chicago's western suburbs, Michael Lefkow, hit me pretty hard. Though we will never know what happened on that sad last day in February 2005, the Milwaukee suicide of his confessed killer at least affords the benefit of sparing the state a trial and us a debate on the value of the death penalty. May the law enforcement investigators redouble their efforts to assure that whoever is responsible has been brought to justice, either on this earth or before the throne of Judgment.

Lefkow's murder (and that of his elderly mother-in-law, Donna Humphrey) calls to mind not only the precariousness of all life, but particularly the sword of Damocles that hangs over the head of those who work for justice. At my small parish, three vestry members and several other active parishioners are lawyers, and speaking only for myself, I have wondered about the mental stability of several clients. Half the time, lawyers are bearers of bad news. The Bible is replete with accounts of how prophets, messengers, emissaries and even the King's Son were murdered for their message. Christ, the ultimate messenger of God's love and mercy, died an even more horrifying and pointless death than Michael Lefkow and Donna Humphrey endured.

In a case fraught with ironies, one of the most perverse is that Bart Ross, the confessed killer, was the sort of client whom Michael represented: down-and-out, marginalized, a victim of the "system."

Together with his grieving widow, Joan (before she became a federal judge), they had been trial lawyers for the Equal Employment Opportunity Commission. But just as Jerusalem, the holy city, was also the abattoir for the prophets, so too is the field of justice for those who work for it.

At Michael's funeral service, which I was blessed to attend, the preacher likened Michael's death to that of Thomas a Becket, the archbishop of Canterbury whom Henry II had murdered in the cathedral. That comparison was drawn when everyone was focusing on an incarcerated white-supremacist as the likely agent provocateur, rather than a garden-variety victim-of-the-system wacko. But even if some link to the Nazi-glorifiers of the world could be proved, the comparison does not serve to glorify Michael's death. The Henry II-Thomas a Becket conflict was a precursor to the Reformation as Henry gained the right to select England's bishops, a right unique in western Christendom where the Pope could barter bishoprics like so many hogs in a pen. That England's Reformation-era bishops, Cranmer, Latimer, Ridley and others, are remembered to this day as giants of the faith and martyrs, while their contemporaries on the Continent are forgotten as so many fools and knaves, shows some redemptive nature to Thomas' untimely demise.

No, Michael's death is no more glorious nor more meaningful than that of any other simple Christian, who worked to live out his faith, who raised children now struggling to make sense of this banality, who loved a woman into their middle years so much that they held hands and shared desk-top lunches, who contributed to the civil society which seems today to be coming unglued. May we still have faith that, as a remnant of believers in a just God, who brought all into existence, and welcomes all who confess the faith of Christ crucified, we may be justified at our hour of judgment, as Michael surely was at his.

[Author's Note: Judge Joan Humphrey Lefkow, who had dismissed Ross' case claiming medical malpractice, was the intended target in this terrible crime. That Michael and her mother died in her stead proves Jesus' dictum: "Greater love hath no man than this, that he should lay down his life for his brother." Maybe that is the ultimate message from this tragedy.]

Aging Gracefully

In the last several months I observed several milestones that, truth be told, I thought I'd never live to see. I celebrated my 50th birthday; with my parents I saw my son graduate from high school in Hawaii not five miles from my father's Marine Corps camp where 57 years earlier he had prepared to invade Japan; and both the suburban parish where I grew up and the inner-city parish where I now worship celebrated their centennials.

It is not that I feared that my life on the edge finally might have caught up with me, or that my son was a candidate for the growing fast-food economy, or that these parishes, as living members of the body of Christ, could not have coped with the changes that the world has flung at them. It is rather that these seemingly disconnected events are given a unity by and through my life in the Church.

Of course, Jesus never reached 50 or had a child. Though called "rabbi" or teacher, he claimed no degree from a school of higher learning. And Herod's Temple, from which Jesus refused to hurl himself to prove His divinity, never reached its centennial before the Romans destroyed it. But Jesus' life, death and resurrection, by which He rebuilt the temple of God's grace toward us, launched a movement that has changed the world by changing lives one by one, day by day.

As far as I can tell, Jesus said next to nothing about the benefits of aging, but His parables are full of accounts of the burdens: the landlord who sent his son to collect the rents; the king who invited many ungrateful guests to his son's wedding; the father who tried to placate his faithful son after the prodigal returned to the fold. Whatever these stories may tell of our relationship to our heavenly Father, they also describe an older man trying to make do with what he has: unruly tenants, disobedient subjects, and distant children.

Some of my friends who have known me for a slug of those 50-plus years find the unity provided by fatherhood and faith, age and acceptance a bit disconcerting. No candidate for sainthood, I can see their point that the Church has covered a multitude of my sins. But having been born and raised in a peace provided by my father's sacrifice, I can only hope that my son can make his own claims to longevity by learning from his father's mistakes.

Contemptuous of those who measured their wisdom by their years and their worth by their piety, Jesus was crucified for us before the infirmities of old age rendered Him less effective. Yet the foundation of the Church he ordained, rebuilt in the three days He lay in the grave, has given me the strength and structure over half-a-century to keep making the effort for him.

Postscript to Self-Offering:

I'm ten years older than I was when I wrote about reaching the half-century mark and in that decade, I've served as senior warden of that 100-year old parish, buried my parents at their 100-year old parish, and served as my community association president after closing down my law practice. Busy times. Yet in those times, I have also had new people come into my life to whom I could serve as silent witness to the peace of God, which passes all understanding. It is only in that service that we find that peace.

REDEMPTION

Introduction:

Though I didn't know it at the time I attended Dartmouth College, there is a direct though distant link between me and John Newton, the author of the world's most famous hymn, "Amazing Grace." Newton was the former English slave trader who turned around his life, working tirelessly to end the slave trade as personal chaplain to the Earl of Dartmouth, Britain's foreign secretary in the mid-1760s. Shortly after the French and Indian War, a young cleric who ran a school for Native Americans in Connecticut sailed to England seeking funds to found a college nearer to Indian territory farther north along the Connecticut River. Through Newton, Eleazar Wheelock met the Earl of Dartmouth, a devoted Christian interested in seeing the Gospel preached to all nations. Hence was founded Dartmouth College, at the intersection of two Indian trails along the New Hampshire-Vermont border. Though some may see this as another example of 18th century British colonialism, indoctrinating the natives to further Britain's global aims against the French, were it simply that, I doubt that the school would have survived. Perhaps now more famous for having spawned the movie "Animal House," Dartmouth's chops as a school which practices what it preaches are undeniable. In true swords-into-plowshares fashion, it welcomes former Marines back from the Middle East, who seek not to blow up the enemy, but to understand him. That is redemption.

The Lesson of the Wounded Healer

"Lord, who sinned? This man or his parents that he was born blind?" the disciples asked of Jesus when they saw the man blind from birth. Jesus answered: "It is not that this man or his parents sinned; he was born blind so that God's power might be displayed in curing him."

Still, the question of who to blame for the human condition remains unresolved despite two millennia of Christians' witness to the power of God to cure those who ask it of Him. Lately, many of us have been asking an updated version of the disciples' question: Was it the blighted condition of South Central Los Angeles that caused the mob to leave Reginald Denny for dead? Or their father's abuse that led the Menendez brothers to their unspeakable shotgun murder of their parents? Bobbitt, Dahmer, Gacy, the list goes on and on.

As a criminal defense lawyer, I confess to a degree of this moral blindness. The accused becomes the victim and I cannot deny that it is an argument that sometimes works. I find some comfort in the Old Testament's answer to the disciples' question, an answer clearly on their minds when they saw the young man: a jealous God visits the sins of the father on the third and fourth generations. And modern science's disclosure of hereditary diseases transmitted from mother to son, father to daughter adds empirical support to the idea that an unconquerable strain of genes causes our own afflictions.

But then I turn back to the Gospel's broader message: that sin has been conquered in the person of Jesus, who simply shows us to take the tools at our hands and offer to heal. While the factions argued who had sinned, the boy remained blind. But once the blind man washed Jesus' spittle-softened mud from his eyes in Siloam's pool he saw Jesus as the light of the world, the Son of Man who had removed both his sin and his blindness.

Perhaps not everyone wants to be healed and certainly not everyone can be the wounded healer. But as the former slave trader turned priest, John Newton, taught us more than 200 years ago, we are all blind without the Risen Lord's amazing grace. That is a lesson that never grows old. And in the long season of Pentecost, as we celebrate the indwelling of the Holy Spirit in the disciples who healed in Jesus' name, let us rejoice in the message that it is not our sin, nor our parents' that caused our blindness, but rather that by faith in God's power, we may be cured.

[Author's note: I wrote this some 20 years ago, and perhaps the names of those events and victims have faded with age. But you could substitute Columbine, the Boston Marathon, Aurora, New Town or any other mind-crunching event in recent history and you'd have the same inquiry: Lord, who sinned? This man or his parents? The answer hasn't changed.]

The Path of Reconciliation

When I was far too young to be spending time away from home, my parents packed me off to a sleep-away camp run by the local Christian college. Undoubtedly grateful for the two week relief from my nine-year-old naughtiness, my parents still rue that decision as I came back believing that I had to read the Bible every day. To say no more, this was strange behavior for a boy who had spent his time memorizing the backs of baseball cards.

Still, perhaps that is why I don't feel uncomfortable around fundamentalists or Bible thumpers or born-agains or those who claim to have been saved. Though we may not agree on everything, they and I can probably agree that all that is necessary for our salvation is contained between Genesis and Revelation. I gladly put my chips on that premise and no other.

But my belief in and preference for the Bible as the root of faith was put in a new light one hot Saturday last summer. I attended a mass men's rally at Soldier Field designed to redirect our lives toward reconciliation: black with white, male with female, parent with child, prisoner with free. There was an odd irony that a locale known for its latter-day gladiatorial contests would yield to the word and will of God. And believing that it is a short road from Jonestown to Nuremburg, I was a bit skeptical of the message.

Reconciliation has been one of the hardest of the Biblical lessons for me to learn, and even harder to practice. In the litmus test world in which I dwell, that divides guilt from innocence, legal from illegal, I have found it much easier to cut off the offending limb and throw it into the fire than try to heal it by prayer, forgiveness and thanksgiving for the differences.

But then it dawned on me: as sure as I am of the premise that the Bible is the foundation of our faith, the Bible is ultimately about the reconciliation of God's creation through His Son, whose death on the cross redeemed us to eternal life. That day took the plank out of my eye.

Witnesses to the Resurrection

Every once in a while, we are witnesses to the resurrection. Not by seeing a Man pierced in hands and side and feet, who comes to us in our hour of need and despair. But in knowing one who was all but dead, and then found new reason for living.

I can't claim that I have ever seen the Wounded Healer. But in the past year, I have seen resurrections of two near to me. The first was my father, a picture of robust health in the 47 years I have known him, but who in the last six months had to stare down cancer and a hip replacement. The second was a friend who for some time skillfully masked a serious addiction.

Both my friend and father had to admit his weakness over the problems he faced before he could continue on. For my father, who had endured Parris Island, raising me, and countless rounds of golf, the pain and complications from the surgery sapped him of his resolve. But thanks to my mother's indomitable spirit and the prayers of many, he has rebounded and hopefully will live another 15 years in active retirement to see the last of his grandchildren graduate from college. And my friend had to overcome that most deceitful of human emotions, denial, before he could accept that he was powerless to combat the problem alone. Confronted by friends and family, he has chosen the road to recovery.

It would be easy, I suppose, to credit these rebirths to the advances of medical science or the power of modern psychology. Undoubtedly, science and psychology played a role in each healing. But viewing each recovery through the lens of the cross, I believe that neither father nor friend would have been made whole if he had not made his own painful pilgrimage to Calvary.

Every once in a while, we become witnesses to the resurrection. And then by the grace of Him who rose from the dead, we too are changed.

The Love that Redeems All Things

Just recently, thanks to my stupidity and blindness, a longstanding love affair ended, and as these things happen, it ended badly. It was not merely the loss of a human connection-something that in my semi-monastic existence comes all too infrequently. It was that this woman helped me to some real insights and revelations about myself, and that she would not be around to help me take the next step. Afraid of being happy in a relationship, I resisted the affections of a woman who truly cared for me.

The surprising thing, though, is how this breakup affected me. As one who had maintained that because of his northern European ancestry, his feelings had been bred out, I felt a profound sense of loss and depression. Out of the depths of despair, I cried out, but no matter where I turned, I could not stop weeping over the mess I had made. Nothing seemed to help, not prayer, not scripture, not friends and not therapy. I felt consigned to a life of alienation and aloneness.

Of course, I grew up in the 50's when feelings were not in vogue. Boys were supposed to stand on their own feet like men and take the slings and arrows of life with stoicism and reserve. The pendulum has swung the other way now, and men gather together to beat drums and chant and get in touch with their inner child and reconnect with the fathers they never knew and the sons they had ignored. For the life of me, I do not know which excess is worse.

From the scriptural accounts, Jesus himself had this problem integrating His personal feelings with His mission. One of the most poignant passages in all the Bible comes in John's eleventh chapter as Jesus first learns of his friend Lazarus' illness, but turns away from the anguish to confront those who had tried to stone him earlier for blasphemy. Diverted for four days in a place far from Lazarus' home, Jesus returns too late to console Lazarus' sisters, Mary and Martha. With their brother now in the tomb, they reproach Jesus for not coming sooner when He could have healed Lazarus. Before revealing His dominion over all things by raising Lazarus from the dead, Jesus weeps.

All religions and most mythologies provide a period of mourning for the loss of a loved one. What distinguishes this narrative from all others is that the Lord of Life, who gave the blind their sight and who taught with the authority of the Father, regretted His own choice. But what comes through even more clearly is that through forgiveness, reconciliation and prayer we all may be raised from the tomb of our own foolish choices to the redemptive grace of fellowship in Christ.

Postscript to Redemption:

My melt-down as I call it lasted for some time and begat a number of follow-on effects, perhaps the subject of another commentary. The point is there is another side and by the grace of God, I found it: not in human relationships which continue to vex me, but in attending to the needs of others: my parents at once self-sufficient but later incapacitated by illness, clients with whom I could empathize, having gone through an ordeal not unlike a lawsuit. Ironically, I may have become a better lawyer. Ultimate redemption however, comes only at the grave when those who have confessed the faith meet Our Lord not as a stranger but as one who has walked our path.

THANKSGIVING

Introduction:

We are always and everywhere to give thanks to Our Lord, even in the pit of our despair. Of course, this is impossible, and a world of praise-the-Lord automatons would be pretty useless. At some point we have to be up and doing, but I think the Christian message is that in the doing we can be, even should be giving thanks to our Creator. I have lived a full life and have been cheated in no respects, but it has not been my doing: it has been the doing of a God who urged me to "do all such good works as He hast prepared for me to walk in," in the words of the post-communion prayer that I committed to memory long ago. Having resolved to follow Jesus Christ as my Lord and Savior when I was confirmed at the tender age of 13, I can say nearly 50 years later that I am thankful that God has never forsaken me, though I'm sure I've exhausted his patience and will likely continue to do so. These essays show that thanksgiving is not so much what we say, but how we say it.

Patching Up the Old

As often as I can, I commute the five miles from home to office by bicycle. Though the health benefits are probably a wash (I trade off inhaling bus fumes and dodging bike-flipping potholes and red-light runners for regular exercise and saving the gym membership fee), I am delivered from the CTA's morning hassles. And I get a chance to collect my thoughts en route while singing a few hymns, something I wouldn't dare inflict on my fellow "L" passengers.

There is one drawback, however. Flat tires. People with no concern for the other guy break bottles and car windows, leaving the shards right in the path of cyclists like me. And for a time, I was getting a lot of flats, all in the same spot on the wheel. Because of my Scottish-bred parsimony I tried to patch the tube rather than replace it. Little good this did on my commute the next day, when I got a new flat. I couldn't figure this out and cursed my wretched fate: doing my best to help the ozone layer, I ended up polluting the verbal atmosphere. I finally solved the problem by selling the bike.

Jesus warned those who tried to patch up old things with the new. "No one sews a patch of unshrunk cloth into a tear in an old garment." He says. "For the patch will pull away from the garment, making the tear worse." Again, Jesus cautions not to put new wine in old wine skins, for the old skins, having stretched as far as they can, will burst as the wine ages and ferments. Luke adds a curious fillip to this teaching found also in Matthew and Mark: "No one after drinking old wine wants the new, for he says, 'The old is better.'"

This cryptic teaching has always puzzled me. Certainly Jesus is offering more than sound bites to the seamstress and the winemaker, but is He saying to throw out the baby with the bathwater? Are we to send old relationships to a Salvation Army recycling bin like so many old clothes? A strange message coming from Him who refused to be made king by force, and rejected all pleas to perform marvelous signs that would herald a new age and Him as the Son of God. But if the old wine is better than the new, what place does the new have?

Christ is of course that which is always new in our old lives. The old garment and old wineskins are merely vessels for that which is truly important to Him: the garment for our earthly bodies which hold the Holy Spirit, and the wineskins for His Blood of the New Covenant. The new bursts through the old, revealing the light of Christ as He continually pours out the Holy Spirit on us. And when my old tire bursts, I am reminded that I cannot remain stationary, but must keep moving forward toward an ever increasing intimacy with Him.

Sowing the Seeds of Faith

My closest friend and companion over the last nine years is not a member of our tradition. Though we have celebrated Christian holidays and enjoyed Christian fellowship, she has not been able to accept the idea that the God who not only created her from nothing also loves her. It seems that more than 20 years ago her father died a slow and painful death and she cannot imagine that a Divine Creator would have subjected him to that suffering. Deprived of her earthly father for wisdom and guidance through young and now mature adulthood, she has stubbornly resisted turning to her Heavenly Father.

Nothing that I have offered my friend, whether from the Old Testament or the New, has answered to her satisfaction the fundamental questions of human existence, pain and death. Nor does the prospect that medical science may have advanced from the data her father's death provided, or that her small and far-flung family grew more tightly knit, or that she has managed on her own for more than half her life. Resolved against any display of God's love in the world, she has built emotional barriers through which no words or actions have passed.

One of the curious things about the Christian faith is that though God calls us (and keeps calling us), he does not force us to listen. Rather, He expects us to respond in love, fully recognizing that our response is always going to fall short. Perhaps that is why He keeps calling us: to understand that we depend on Him, and not on ourselves.

I thought about the response each of us gives to God's call when I heard again the story of the rich young ruler who asked Jesus what he must do to inherit eternal life. This story is filled with theological significance on a host of levels. And that it appears almost word-for-word at precisely the same point in three Gospels gives compelling evidence that Jesus was as he said, the Son of God. What makes the story especially poignant though is not the camel-through-the-eye-of-the-needle metaphor, nor the promise of hundred-fold return of all that his followers had left behind to follow Jesus. No, its poignancy lies in the fact that Jesus knew this man's longings in life, and spoke to them. The ruler, feeling that Jesus had hit him where he lived, turned away sad.

As for my friend, the Lord whom I follow is real, though not always responsive in a way that I can understand or explain. But what her doubt has shown me is as important as any faith: for though she may not believe that she too is part of God's plan, her doubt still sows the seeds of faith, and God uses her through me and others to reveal His glory in the world.

Recognizing the Stranger

Every once in a while, I am haunted by a memory of seeing someone I vaguely know and thinking, "there but for the grace of God, go I." About eight years ago, I was playing golf with my father. The caddy looked familiar, but for the life of me, I could not place him. He was disheveled, almost unkempt, with odd mannerisms. But he knew the distances to the hole and what club I should hit. Then on about the 14th hole, it dawned on me: we had been at the same high school, even members of the same gymnastics team. How our paths had diverged since then: I to college and professional school; he to the school of hard knocks, carrying my golf bag. I later learned that he may have been in a car accident or been incapacitated by service in Vietnam, or perhaps it was drugs or alcohol or just the ennui of life.

I was reminded of this event on re-reading the story of Jesus on the road to Emmaus. Two of Jesus' disciples, in a state of confusion after the death of their Lord and the disappearance of His Body, were walking on a road when a stranger came up and asked them what they were talking about. The disciples did not recognize Jesus and inquired whether he was just a visitor to Jerusalem as if that might explain his ignorance of the events of the last several days. They then recounted His death and the resurrection vision of angels seen by the women who had gone to the tomb. Still not perceiving the Stranger as the Lord, the disciples invited Him on to supper. It was only after Jesus broke the bread, blessed it and gave it to them that the disciples came to realize that the Stranger was the Lord in their midst, known to them in the breaking of the bread.

I confess that this post-resurrection story has always given me the most difficulty. The miracle of the resurrection is explicable to the incredulous if you accept an Omnipotent Creator. From there, it is just a small step to believe that Jesus somehow appeared through a locked door to reconcile a doubting Thomas. But flesh-and-blood disciples failing to to recognize a flesh-and-blood Jesus after having seen him teach and heal for three years? No way. Rational explanations fail: Could His face and form have been so distorted on the cross that His students could not see their teacher? Did His last gasp for a God who had forsaken Him alter his voice? Nothing truly suffices.

But then I remember my own failure of recognition on the golf course long ago. And I am reminded of other miraculous recognitions: St. Francis' seeing the face of Jesus in that of a leper to whom he was giving alms. St. Augustine's recognition when he thought about stealing apples from a neighbor's tree that he, too, was a sinner. Alexander Solzhenitsyn's prison-inspired conclusion that the line between good and evil crosses every human heart. Even Peter's confession to Jesus that He was not John the Baptist or a prophet reincarnate, but the Christ, the Son of the Living God, was a miracle. Jesus tells Peter: "For this was not revealed to you by man but by my Father in heaven."

Every once in a while I am haunted by the memory that I failed to recognize a stranger whom I once knew. And then I remember that the stranger has failed to recognize me.

[Author's note: Perhaps my favorite work of literature is Albert Camus' *The Stranger*. This manifesto of existentialism by an atheist Nobel prize winner stands as a powerful argument against any notion that our lives have meaning or purpose. I tremble as I think of the absurdity of Meursault, *The Stranger's* hero, failing to defend himself against a murder charge that he could have beaten. But then I remember that we are all strangers one to another until we recognize that we are all brothers and sisters in a Lord who also refused to defend himself.]

The Gifts of the Spirit

Lately it seems I've met a number of people who say they are "spiritual" without being "religious." When I ask them to explain, they say they have an "inner life," a "higher power," and a "spiritual awareness," all without the guilt and bad memories they associate with organized religion and its rituals and requirements. Instead they light candles or chant, or hold hands in a circle or simply walk alone in the woods, trying to "feel" the presence of a power outside themselves.

I find this claim of "spirit" without "religion" interesting. Religion of course is a tie among others and to God. For better or for worse, God has called us into a community, and religion with all its rules tells us where and how we fit in. But when I ask these folks what the spirits are saying if they do not point to God and help us understand our role in His Kingdom, they politely change the subject or end the conversation entirely.

Few Christians talk these days of the Holy Spirit, the Lord and Giver of Life, who has spoken through the prophets, as we say, or perhaps better yet, the Advocate, the Spirit of Truth as Jesus promised that He would send His disciples the night before He died. We don't even hear of politicians with "charisma" any more, yet that word hearkens back to the gifts of the Spirit of which St. Paul wrote. Yet 20 centuries ago, the Spirit was the talk of the town. Peter and Stephen were full of the Spirit when they preached to the Sanhedrin, answering charges of blasphemy. The Spirit let Stephen see Jesus at the right hand of God as he was being stoned. And as He died, Jesus publicly committed His Spirit into the hand of the Father.

Jesus likened the Spirit to wind, not knowing where it blows or whence it comes. Yet over time the purpose of the Spirit is clear: to stand by us when we need support, to nudge us when we need incentive, and to bring new life to us when we need refreshment. Many is the time that I have been ready to throw in the towel only to have some person come into my life or some event happen that can only be explained by the power of the Spirit. At least as importantly, on those rare occasions when I feel that I am acting as God would have me, serving others outside of myself, a profound sense of harmony with all the world overcomes me.

But like wind, which needs vanes to be harnessed so that mills can grind the grain, the Spirit works only with those willing to listen. I pray that my friends who commune with spirits open their ears to the Holy Spirit who has brought them to the place they now are in, so that they may understand that God as Spirit draws them ever closer to the people of His communion.

The Widow's Gift

Whether it's urban paranoia, Scottish-bred parsimony, or just the fact that an ATM is always handy, I never carry around a lot of cash with me. Unsurprisingly, therefore, I sometimes find myself in church a bit short. And so it happened early one Sunday morning that I arrived not having written a check for my pledge, and having just one dead president in my pocket which was more than I wanted to put in the plate. Just my luck that the Gospel that Sunday was the familiar story of the rich men and the widow. When Jesus saw her put two copper coins into the temple treasury, He said that the widow's gift was worth more than the others' because she gave all she had out of her poverty.

Rather than throw caution to the wind and put in all I had, however, hoping that the cash machine gods would later look favorably on me, I shunned the plate that day. I wish I could say that I have made it up in subsequent offerings.

Like many I suspect, I spend far too much of my time worrying about money. Though I have been richly blessed, and have never wanted for anything, it seems that I am always checking bank balances and bill clips, bills and IRA statements. But even if my name were Rockefeller, I doubt that I would live any more extravagantly than I do now. Grateful for what I have, I would find it difficult to be a good steward over more.

A wise man once told me that Jesus preached more about our relationship to wealth than anything else. I find this curious for several reasons. With only a tunic for His executioners to cast lots over, Jesus was hardly wealthy by earthly measure. His descent from the kingly line of Solomon and David, not the ascetic line of Elijah and Moses, might have suggested a cavalier attitude toward the material world. And having forsaken the reward of all earthly power and dominion for worshiping Satan, Jesus might have left it at that, expecting believers in Him to follow the way of denial.

But being fully human, Jesus also knew that where our treasure is, there are our hearts. Understanding that we will never be satisfied with our success and stature, wealth and worldly attainment, He taught us by word and deed as clear as the widow's offering that all that we have is what we have given away, from God's graciousness to us, in the service of others.

Freedom and Restraint

For several months now, I've been trying to figure out why the movie *A River Runs Through It* moved me more than any film since *Chariots of Fire*. Was it the uncanny resemblance to my life shown in technicolor? Like Norman Maclean, I went to Dartmouth College having been told I could go anywhere I wanted and like him, I know how my parents sacrificed to send me there. My grandmother's name was Jessie, like Maclean's mother, and my grandfather was a fisherman in Western rivers. A second cousin is a Presbyterian minister who has spent most of his life preaching in near pagan cultures. I even spend part of my time trying to teach writing in Chicago.

Though few others with whom I've talked about the movie share such points of tangency, still they have been moved. Was it the magnificent scenery of Montana's skyline, the poignancy of a young man's rough death, or the enigma of all father–son relationships? Was it the metaphor of a river for our lives, the rapids yielding bounty amidst danger, the trout's leap for the fly giving beauty and meaning to our struggle to survive?

Perhaps, but there must be more. In today's cultural war pitting the popular elite of Hollywood against the "traditional values" of Main Street, it is encouraging that a movie could be made that does more than pander. While *A River Runs Through It* may not signal a shift of Hollywood's focus any more than any other movie showing something beyond sex and violence, it does sound a still small voice of decency in a world which too often lacks it.

But as they view the movie, Christians might consider the subtle themes of freedom and restraint: the freedom of a river on its course, restrained by the physical force of gravity within the canyon walls, is reflected in our freedom to choose how we live, restrained by God's moral force.

My life may not completely imitate the art of Norman Maclean as translated to celluloid by Robert Redford. But I can be glad that, as a Christian, the river running through it is God's moral force impressed on me by my ancestors.

[Author's Note: Since I wrote this many years ago, I have come to know Norman Maclean's daughter through a professional association. She works to free the innocent and compensate those wrongfully convicted. And I saw the movie again for the first time since it was released. The final scene of an elderly Maclean tying a fly in the "half-light of the canyon with the sounds of the Big Black Foot River cut by the world's great flood running over rocks from the basement of time" again brought tears to my eyes.]

Postscript to Thanksgiving:

Martin Luther taught that it was by faith in Christ alone that we are saved, and I believe that beyond my ability to express. Part of me, however, would prefer that I could earn my way or buy my way to salvation, because that would be a benchmark that I could shoot for: so many dollars given or deeds done. Yet knowing myself, that wouldn't be enough; I'd still want to do more or be more or give more. St. Paul perhaps said it best: complaining about the "thorn in his flesh" with which "a messenger of Satan" had tormented him, Paul quoted God: "My grace is sufficient for you, for my power is made perfect in weakness." The Christian message through 20 centuries is that God's power is made perfect in our weakness, and for that we must be thankful, for it is in our weakness that we find a God who gives us reason to give thanks.

LITURGY

Introduction:

I grew up in what was called a "morning prayer" parish in which
the focus was the recitative chants that I can still recite if not quite
sing. Labeled with Latin names that sparked my interest in foreign
languages, these chants were drawn from Biblical texts that I suspect
have now been largely forgotten: "O be joyful in the Lord all ye
lands"; "Blessed be the Lord God of Israel; for he hath visited and
redeemed his people." Many years ago, the church I have attended
switched to an all-communion, all the time schedule which for better
or worse has omitted these ancient texts. Still, the order of service, if
done right and reverently, conveys a sense of the mystery of our faith:
that in the simple gifts of bread and wine, we are transformed into
living members of the Body of Christ. These essays try to animate
that sense of mystery, combined with the tangible reality of our
being fed, not by bread alone, but by every word that comes from
the mouth of the Father.

The Cup of Salvation

A few months ago, I started back as a chalice bearer at the early morning service I have been attending for a while. As a persistent back-bencher (and late arrival) at several parishes for the last 10 years, it is something of a leap for me once again to face the congregation from behind the rail and assist in the holy meal which links us to Our Lord. Consistent with my ministry as a layperson, however, I do not wear vestments, and I'm sure my mother would recoil in horror to learn that I have been seen assisting at the altar wearing shorts in a sanctuary air-conditioned through clerestory windows. I defend my habit (pun intended) by saying that way the perspiration which would otherwise bead my brow is less likely to drop into the chalice.

The priesthood of all believers is a watchword of our faith sealed with our baptism, and I am glad that the rector whom I assist is willing to accommodate my sartorial preferences. Of course the age is less formal than when I grew up singing in cassock and cotta in a boys' choir. Perhaps because I didn't like that dress, I never advanced to acolyte or adult choir. But I admit that it is a far cry from the ancient vestments I spurned to the casual Sunday attire I now sport.

The form of our worship is one of Anglican Christendom's great gifts to the world. Non-believers who have accompanied me to church have universally praised the language and even the ceremony. Words like "oblation" and "intercession," almost extinct from our collective vocabulary, take on meaning when used to describe the sacrifice which we commemorate each week. The blessing of simple elements, gifts from the congregation, returned as holy food and drink to waiting believers, becomes one of faith's great mysteries.

Though my dress may not reflect it, I honor the ancients in faith by reciting the prayer drawn from the Reformation compromise: "The blood of our Lord Jesus Christ, which was shed for thee, preserve thy body and soul unto everlasting life. Drink this in remembrance that Christ's blood was shed for thee, and be thankful." Evoking both our temporal need for forgiveness and our spiritual yearning for life eternal, these words convey with the substance of our faith our hope for union with the One whose love for us bore all.

Our holy communion may not seem like much to the non-believer. But to this casually-clad chalice bearer, it is the visible sign that what we believe is not so much a doctrine, but a faith: that God is present with us in all things, and most particularly when we are fed with words of grace.

The Paradox of Prayer

When I was growing up in church, rather than listen to the sermons to try to make sense of them, I devoted my mental energy to memorizing the prayers and collects, confessions and thanksgivings. To this day, I can recite many once-familiar prayers from the old prayer book. But this does me little good these days as the church powers trumped me, changing the prayer book, and eliminating many of my favorite words and expressions. Phrases like "thine inestimable love," "our souls washed through His most precious Blood," and "feed on Him in thy heart, by faith with thanksgiving," have sadly fallen out of our Christian consciousness.

I had an ulterior motive in memorizing large chunks of small type. If only I could recite the collect of the week, I would pass the next day's test or perform well in that week's athletic contest or get into the college I had longed for. For some reason, I haven't been able to shake this notion 30 years later. But instead of praying about tests and games, I pray about checks and mail, bills and clean bills of health.

Seeking to know and do God's will has seldom been the object of this quest. In fairness, I was hoping that God would ratify what I wanted to do, and likely was going to do anyway. And I suppose it is a wonder that God has not said, "Enough already. You've passed those tests, graduated from college, paid your bills and still managed to make a shambles of everything."

Prayer is one of those paradoxes of the Christian faith. We are told to pray unceasingly, always giving thanks for our blessings. As if prayer pays the rent or harvests the crops. And we are told to pray not that our will be done, but God's. As if we have no role to play in ushering in God's kingdom. But the paradox is that in praying that God's will be done, He sees to it that we have work and food. In thanking God for our blessings, He sees to it that others are there when we need them.

I have lived long enough to recognize that when I think that I am acting in conformance with God's will, He has a curious though emphatic way of telling me otherwise. And in the 30-plus years since I began committing our common prayer to memory, I have learned to commit myself to the truth that God's will is done, not merely in my life, but in the lives of all for whom I pray.

Humbling Ourselves Before God

Like many, I was relieved and gratified when the Bulls won their 1998 championship. Relieved that after so much hype and expectation, that decade's version of "the best team ever" lived up to its reputation. Gratified that once again, talented individuals, led by a coach with a Christian mystic's insight, would sacrifice their personal interests to the common good.

Jordan, Pippen, Rodman, Kukoc, Longley and the rest: could anyone imagine a more diverse group? Forget that they come from three continents and two planets. One wants to wrestle, another play golf and baseball, another surf. Yet over a long season, they passed off, rebounded and helped out on defense all to the idea that in teamwork lies success.

The parallel is imperfect, but the early Church felt many of the same divergent pressures. Do we require circumcision and ritual cleanliness? Do we stay in Jerusalem or move out? Do we expect Christ's imminent return or in God's good time? It took the better part of three centuries before the Church resolved these issues, and then only for a time. These questions have a tendency to crop up like weeds in a well-tended field. You don't know where they come from, and yet all of a sudden they are there.

By the early accounts, Paul and Peter were as difficult as Rodman and Pippen. Both Paul (in Galatians) and Luke (in Acts) record how Peter first preached God's salvation through Christ to the Gentiles in Antioch, then recanted that position, believing that the Gentiles had to be circumcised to become Christians. Paul confronted Peter, and proved to him that those who were Jews by birth could not be justified by observing the law but by faith in Christ. If that were true of the Jews, how could more be expected of the Gentiles?

Understandably, Peter does not recount this dispute in his two brief epistles. But aware of his tendency toward absolutism, Peter condemned false teachers and prophets who introduced destructive heresies, even denying the sovereign Lord whose blood on the cross redeemed them. Despite the passage of years his words ring true: "Humble yourselves under God's mighty hand, that He may lift you up in due time. Resist the devil, standing firm in your faith, because you know that your brothers throughout the world are undergoing the same kind of sufferings." Reconciled to the truth that Christ came into the world to save all sinners, in his later years Peter praised Paul's teaching that our Lord's patience means salvation for all who believe in Him. Patience in suffering; humility before God; resisting evil; firmness in the faith; leading to salvation for all. Taking a lesson from the Bulls, Christians might well learn that in working for the common good we find our most mature expression of our individuality.

The Music of God's Angels

Though I am a member of, and even a regular attendee at the parish closest to my home, I spend a fair number of Sundays and holidays worshiping at other churches. Sometimes, these are familiar places or those that have meant something to me in the past. Occasionally, however, these are completely new and different that I happen on as if by accident. It is at these new stops along my spiritual journey where I often find the most meaningful experiences.

This past year, I shared God's fellowship with His people at two new places. Both were in a neighborhood I don't frequent. And though my parish is as diverse as any you're likely to find, at each of these services, as a white male, I was in a distinct minority.

Gone also were the organ and vested choir to which I've become accustomed. At one service, they were replaced by an older man playing a soprano saxophone; at another, they were replaced by a pianist accompanying a soloist singing hymns they had composed.

Church music has touched me in a way that no earthly device has. This has always puzzled me, as I have something of a tin ear, and gave up trying to sing on key when my voice changed. But one of the proofs that God exists has been that the words and melodies I hear in churches near and far resonate not only in my cracking voice, but in my moistened tear ducts. Somehow, the God-shaped hole in my heart is filled when I hear the hymns that sing the story of the Creator who took human form.

Somehow, too, God finds me at these out-of-the-way places I happen on as if by accident. I know this because He has spoken to me through His angels, whose music moves me to tears.

By Whose Authority?

People who know me only casually find it absolutely incredible that I write articles for the religious press. After all, I never attended seminary or even took a college-level theology course, I have at best a spotty knowledge of the Bible, and as a lawyer by profession, I am paid to argue *ad nauseam*. This is not to mention a personal life in perpetual turmoil, tenuous relationships with my family and the rest of humanity, and a vocabulary I'm ashamed to admit more French than the Queen's English.

Of course, I can come up with plenty of explanations for the cognitive dissonance: that God needs sinners like me to point others the way to Him; that we have all sinned and nobody can stand righteous before God; that the Bible and even secular history record countless instances of lives dramatically changed by God's message of redemption. But on hearing this, my casual acquaintances wonder when they are going to see the outward and visible signs of my inward and spiritual grace. They are not persuaded when I say that they should have seen me way back when.

Some find the Christian attitude toward sin off-putting. If we can't be righteous enough to earn recognition before God, then what's the point of even trying? Or more pointedly, how can the faith claim any moral legitimacy when it embraces sinners like me? Why not just observe the state's laws and be done with it? Better yet, why not try to trim the state's laws to see how much we can get away with? If my sins are forgiven, then what's to stop me from committing them again and again?

These questions defy easy answers. To respond that this is cynicism which mocks God or invites a cheap grace not worthy of the Redeemer's suffering makes sense only if you believe that a Creator sent His Son to die for us in obedience to His will. If you don't buy into that concept, you can reason your way to anything.

Before He died, Jesus faced the same measure of disaffection with His teachings. Grumbling when they heard that only Jesus was the bread of life, His disciples reproached Him for not performing miraculous signs to prove His authority. Jesus responded that only those who ate of His flesh should have His gift of life eternal. After some had left because they had found this road too hard, Jesus asked the remaining twelve whether they too wanted to leave. Peter's simple reply (as befits a fisherman), has confounded the scholars through the ages: "Lord, to whom shall we go? You alone have the words of eternal life." In a way that I can scarcely begin to describe, God has made it plain that these words are true.

Postscript to Liturgy:

Many years ago, I went on my first religious retreat. This was not quite voluntary; I was doing it out of a sense of obligation to my then wife in an effort to save a marriage that, truth be told, was misbegotten. The retreat was held at a monastery, not the sort of place that I frequent, and except for what we were allowed to say during the several services each day, we were supposed to maintain silence, quite a chore for someone who talked for a living. On the third day of this exercise during the communion service that I had heard 1,000 times before tears started streaming down my face, uncontrollably. I was not sobbing, not feeling remorse or pain, simply experiencing what some religious call the "gift of tears," an ecstatic sense of harmony with your creator. The philosophically-inclined would not take this as a proof of God's existence, but I do.

FAITH

Introduction:

As much as Christianity is a religion, which ties us one another and to the divine; as much as it is a liturgy, with works done in sacrifice or remembrance; as much as it is a theology, a system of beliefs and philosophical structures that withstand rigorous inquiry; it is more a faith, a simple hope that God loves us and will never forsake us. These essays try as I might to explain my faith.

The Faith That Leads Us Home

"Justification by faith," my friend, a lapsed Catholic, asked. "What does it mean?" I tried to explain to her St. Paul's Epistle to the Romans; the faith that led the Jewish patriarchs; that faith is the substance of things hoped for, the evidence of things unseen; Martin Luther and the 95 theses. I might as well have read her a doctoral dissertation.

And then last summer, I was with my 11-year old son standing in line to ride the latest roller coaster at Great America. When I was his age, you couldn't get me anywhere near the ones at Riverview Park, and this was before the multiple loop and stand-up varieties that we have now. My son, who must have some adventurous genes, has loved the scariest of them since he was tall enough to ride. But some 20 years ago, I somehow conquered my fear of free-falls and inverted suspension. I don't quite remember how this came about, but I must have come to believe that if others had survived, so could I. And now I can share the faith-building experience of a roller coaster ride with my son.

Of course, I have had faith experiences more significant than a roller coaster ride since that first one 20 years ago. Job changes and moves half-way across the country, parenthood and my grandparents' deaths, bar exams and mad dashes to O'Hare have all strengthened my belief that the God who created me has also sustained me no matter how far I've strayed. And this, I suppose is the other half of my friend's question. Justification by faith. How could we be made just simply by believing?

In the summer blockbuster Apollo 13, Jim Lovell (played by Tom Hanks) answered a reporter's question about any superstitious fears borne of the mission's number. Early in Lovell's career as a Navy fighter pilot, he explained, the cockpit lights went out on his return from a night-time combat mission. He could not read the gauges to try an instrument approach to the carrier which had gone dark so as not to attract enemy fire. Lovell was literally flying blind in the darkness of the Pacific. And then, when he looked down for a place to ditch his plane, he saw the fluorescent green of the algae stirred up in the wake of a large ship—his carrier. Knowing that somehow there would be a way, Lovell survived to captain the mission that captured our prayers 25 years ago.

If anyone has the right to be proud of his accomplishments, I suppose it would be Jim Lovell. But this vignette showed the truth that not by our merits are we justified before God, but by the simple faith that with Him, there will be a way.

Struggling with a Smile

One afternoon my infant son re-enacted the myth of Sisyphus. Remember Sisyphus? He was the mythical Greek who, for some transgression against the gods, was sentenced to an afterlife of rolling a rock up a hill, only to trip and have it roll down before he reached the top. Then he would have to roll the rock back up again in an endless succession of effort and frustration.

My son was doing something like that on the playground. I put him on the slide and as he got down, he'd try to crawl back up. Since he was only nine-and-a-half months old, he had a hard time getting up more than a couple of feet before he'd turn around, come down and start his ascent all over again.

As frustrating as this was to watch (and perhaps as frightening), Adam was having a wonderful time, laughing and babbling with obvious delight. He didn't care that he couldn't reach the top. He was enjoying just crawling up and sliding down.

Adam's going up and down the slide, never quite reaching the top, but struggling nevertheless, is similar to our lives. Some of us have fun in this effort, others are burned out by it, others see no point to it, but do it to pay the rent or because nothing else is available. My son taught me that the attitude is what counts. He was having fun even though he was doing something he couldn't understand.

Few of us will understand what our callings in life are, let alone realize them. Yet each of us will struggle as we pursue our perceptions of those callings: in jobs, relationships, recreation. We will certainly know frustration: some of us may know fulfillment. But in between frustration and fulfillment is a large area where most of us will live most of our lives. How to live is the question.

Adam showed me that it isn't necessary to understand my calling to enjoy what I am doing. The simple fact of having something to do is cause in itself for rejoicing. Whether life is perceived as frustrating or fulfilling is completely beside the point. We have life now and we can enjoy it.

Unlike Sisyphus, however, those of us who roll rocks up the hill have something more to look forward to than an eternity of frustration. Jesus promised that we could join Him in paradise if we believe in Him, irrespective of our earthly lives, work and station. More than that, He freed us from concerns over the frustrations of this life by letting us enjoy it.

Adam enjoyed life that afternoon on the slide, frustrating as it was. He taught me a lesson.

[Author's note: This was my first essay of a religious vein published, and it was the last for several years as I concentrated on practicing law in a new city. Somehow, the bug had bit me, and the essays in this book are the result. Nearly 30 years after this was published, I can't be certain that I have found my calling or fulfillment. What I can say is that God has kept me from falling off the slide, and giving into frustration.]

The Light that Shows True Faith

For some reason, my law practice seems to hit the doldrums between Thanksgiving and New Year's, so for several years, I have taken a part-time position at one of Chicago's leading department stores. It beat staring at the walls waiting for the phone to ring, and besides, in the spirit of the holidays, I was able to share some of these essays with fellow workers who were not likely to be reading these pages. Just as important, this was the store where my sisters and I not only met Santa Claus during annual pilgrimages, but also where we learned to care for others less fortunate by dropping part of our hard-earned allowances into the Salvation Army kettles outside.

Many in the culture decry the "commercialization" of Christmas. Given our contentious age, others then argue that this is what Christ would want were He to return in our time: gift-giving, celebrations of the joy of life, families' smoothing over their differences, even welcoming the occasional stranger. I can't resolve this debate, which in some way rages inside each of us. Did selling out to commercial interests by trying to ratchet up sales so that I could pay my own bills compromise my ability to share my faith?

The Lord whose birth we celebrate at this time held few illusions about our gift for rationalizing our actions. He lambasted lawyers who laid burdens on those they claimed to serve and physicians who could not heal themselves. He doubted the motives of those who came to Him and criticized those He healed when they showed no gratitude. Yet when confronted with true faith, typically from an outsider to His culture—the Roman centurion who asked Jesus to heal his servant, Zaccheus the tax collector who climbed a tree to see Jesus, the Samaritan woman at Jacob's well who asked Jesus for living water—He showed the generosity of His Father's gifts to all of us.

Modern department stores take on the trappings of ancient temples: ornament and excitement, refreshment and re-connection with our early memories. Finding Christ amidst the trappings may be hard. But in the hustle and bustle, I try to remember that His Birth has delivered me from my day-to-day concerns over fees and failings, airline schedules and conflicts over holiday parties. And I try to show those who have come to the temple of commerce to trade in God's abundance that the Light who came through the darkest hours of our souls shines brighter than those on any tree or display.

Postscript to Faith:

In the words of the Epistle to the Hebrews, faith is the substance of things hoped for, the evidence of things not seen. Faith can be manifest in many things: sacrifice, dedication, resolve, commitment, but it is manifest most in a belief that Christ Jesus came into the world to save sinners. In that belief is found our hope for salvation not seen in a kingdom on a distant shore. We will all get there soon enough.

SEASONS

Introduction:

The church year is divided into seasons, designed to arrange the message of the Gospel to our temporal existence once agrarian or pastoral. But the Church's origin in the northern hemisphere puts its seasons out of whack in Australia, or Argentina, South Africa or Sumatra. While I have never been south of the equator let alone worshiped there, I can only imagine what it is like to celebrate Christmas during the summer solstice, or Easter during the harvest. But the Church's roots in a time when people depended entirely on the will of God to send rains in due course does not make those seasons less relevant now when we can get fresh produce from halfway around the world. If anything, that history shows God's love for us by not requiring us to adapt to creation, but by adapting creation to us.

Preparing for a Breakthrough

On a desolate December Sunday afternoon three years ago, a friend and I were wandering around one of Chicago's emerging yuppie neighborhoods. As we admired the rows of Victorian-style stone houses along the boulevard lined with leaf-barren trees, we happened on a small Gothic church. It was somewhat out of place in that neighborhood, which featured storefront chapels with signs in Spanish. But from inside, we heard the ethereal sounds of an organ. Was the choir practicing?

Curious, and as much in need of physical warmth as spiritual comfort, we went inside, and found ourselves amidst an Advent celebration singing hymns and hearing lessons I have known since my childhood. We stayed a while, but the experience was somewhat lost on my friend, who is not a Christian. So we left to continue our excursion before it became too dark to see more stone buildings fronting other tree-lined boulevards.

I remembered this brief but holy moment while reading one of the Advent lessons about John the Baptist. How many who heard his message prepared the way of the Lord in their hearts, and how many went back to their business?

Perhaps the answer to us is meaningless. Enough had their hearts broken by John's call for repentance so that they could be open to God's love for us shown in the Word Made Flesh, reconciling us to the Father. Christ came into the world without so much as a thought from any of us. He broke through the desolation of all our

Decembers by asking us to spend a few moments with Him, in a stone church or in a storefront chapel, in a soup kitchen or in a shelter.

I vowed to return to that church which lies some distance from my house, a vow I recently kept. Curious, I thought, that was the vow that Christ made and which we look forward this season to His keeping.

Trying to Enter Through
the Narrow Door

One recent Lent, I resolved to give up a popular game that came pre-loaded with my personal computer. Though reasonably harmless, this game was taking up time that I should have spent writing briefs or developing more clients. After dutifully observing my Lenten discipline from Ash Wednesday through the next Sunday, I fell into the temptation of trying to outwit the machine. My resolution once broken, I made no effort to rehabilitate myself, awaiting divine indictment for the offense of killing time.

It has become a fashion these days not to give something up for Lent like candy or desserts, but to take on something new, perhaps a prayer regimen, or a Bible study, or an extra worship service, or working at a soup kitchen. I suppose that this is in keeping with the popular culture, which tells us that we can never have enough or do enough or live enough and what better way to satisfy those cravings than to try to do more?

Jesus warned those who wanted to take the easy road to eternal life. "Try to enter through the narrow door," He told his followers. But He also rebuked those who thought that God's righteousness could be earned, and those who renounced all of life's pleasures. St. Paul likewise urged the early Christians to live in moderation. Wise words perhaps to those who thought that with wine came truth and girth suggested wealth, but scarcely earth-shattering these days when we measure our cholesterol as often as our bank accounts. To those who practice moderation anyway, it may seem pointless to forgo something. Perhaps it would be better if we added a new discipline or regimen to our daily lives. Then at least we could look back on the 40 days and see if we had learned or accomplished something.

I have no answer for this dilemma. Even though my metabolism has slowed to keep pace with my sedentary lifestyle, I haven't tried to fast for a number of years, even on Ash Wednesday or Good Friday. And I can't bear the thought of taking on an added chore. I already have plenty to do even if I waste too much time getting it done. And joining a 12-step program for computer game addicts seems too facile: admitting I'm powerless over the game doesn't stop me from clicking it on.

But I draw comfort that, unlike John the Baptist who came neither eating nor drinking, Christ ate with tax collectors and drank with publicans. This Lent, I'll remember that as I try to stay away from my computer game.

The Faith that Connects Us

One of the wonderful things about growing up in the Church and staying with it all these years is seeing the connections over time with others whose Christian paths have crossed mine. The young curate, who blessed my Boy Scout God & Country award in 1966, has spent his entire career in the Chicago diocese, faithfully serving several parishes for long stretches. We see each other now and then at church functions, and marvel that we still remember the role that we played in each other's lives.

A 16-year-old high schooler who heard me lecture on Constitutional law many years ago was inspired to go to law school. After passing the bar, he clerked for a devoted churchman who invited him to sing in his church's choir. That led him down the path to seek holy orders. Both that churchman—a leading federal judge—and I attended that young man's ordination several years ago. One of the recent candidates for bishop in our diocese visited me in a New York hospital when I was recovering from surgery nearly 20 years ago, and he was in his first parish job. And a young doctor, who on reading my essays first began to consider herself a child of God, was confirmed last year in the Anglican communion, radiating the light of Christ as no one I had ever seen. She recently married an Episcopal priest and now affectionately refers to herself as the church lady. The list goes on.

I thought about these connections one recent celebration of All Saints Day. Though popularly remembered as the day we recover from Halloween, All Saints Day is actually one of our oldest church celebrations. What sets it apart from others, at least for me, is that rather than commemorate the church giants whose bold gestures and grand visions have built the structure of our faith, All Saints celebrates those whose quiet devotion and steadfast striving have given the texture and pattern, color and strength to the Christian experience.

"And some there be, which have no memorial; who are perished, as though they had never been; and they are become as though they had never been born; and their children after them," the passage from Ecclesiasticus for All Saints Day reads. "But these were merciful men, whose righteousness hath not been forgotten. With their seed shall continually remain a good inheritance, and their children are within the covenant." The least of my brothers and sisters play the starring roles in God's holy pageant.

Staying within the Church covenant has had its costs and consequences over these years. I meet people I do not like, and I often find out, after a moment of theological insight, that I don't like myself too much either. But the connections to the faith forged over decades of common prayer and holy communion have given me the strength and courage to continue, secure in the knowledge that the road where I have met those whom God has placed in my path leads to the heavenly city where we will all be welcomed and find a place at God's eternal banquet.

[Author's Note: The priest who blessed my God and Country award went to his eternal reward several years ago. I went to his funeral and there re-connected, after an absence of 40 years, with a man with whom I had grown up, and also met a woman who had known my aunt when they were both young living on a country road near the Fox River in Illinois. The connections continued. And that lawyer-turned-priest recently returned to the practice of law, I understand. I tried to warn him about the perils of the priesthood and said that the church needs dedicated laymen before he sought holy orders, but like most, he wouldn't listen to me.]

Holy Places, Holy Times

It seems that fall is a time of reflection and lately, I've been considering holy places and holy times in my life. I can't say what causes this, whether it is advancing age or some divine clock inspiring me in my middle years, but it was not so long ago that fall was a time for beginnings: new schools, new jobs, and as a die hard Bears fan, a new football season. Now, I look forward to higher heating bills and the mercurochrome stigmata on hands blistered by raking leaves.

The season's scriptures also cause reflection. "What is the greatest commandment?" the Sadducee asked Jesus. Responding with the Hebrew Kaddish, "Hear, O Israel," Jesus instead gave two: Loving God with all your heart, and loving your neighbor as yourself. But how many times have I failed to fulfill these commandments? Every time I pass a homeless person or start an argument, drop a dollar in the plate instead of ten.

But there must be more than the perpetual guilt trip implicit in this passage. The Sadducee acknowledged that loving God and your neighbor were more important than burnt offerings and sacrifices. Jesus then silenced the critics who had tried to trick him throughout his ministry by stating that the Sadducee was close to the kingdom of God. Although Jesus doesn't say why, I suspect that it was because the Sadducee realized that no matter what we did, it would never be enough. It is better that our prayers be our questions, and our work be our worship.

When I heard this passage again, I was reminded of my college president's farewell: "Men of Dartmouth (we were all men then), you are your brother's keeper, and the world is your brother." Few who knew me then would say that my college years were spent in holy pursuits at a place set apart for God (though that is why it had been founded). But as that college president suggested, because I was at that place, at that time, I have traveled to new places that have become holy.

We may not recognize the places in our lives as holy when we are there, but hopefully by the time the fall comes around, we will.

The Angels of Our Lives

Christmas is a time when we think of angels: Gabriel, who announced Jesus' birth to Mary; the angel who told Joseph not to fear that his betrothed had conceived of the Holy Spirit; the angels who greeted the shepherds with news of Jesus' birth. Lately, I've been thinking of the angels of my life. Not the sort with wings and halos and harps of gold, but those people who have come into my life at just the right moment with a message that I needed to hear, and have even, occasionally, heeded.

In the early 1980s, when I was a young lawyer in New York struggling for material success and professional recognition, the first woman priest I ever heard preach said that my path was not that of the Christian. Telling how Gideon, the Old Testament leader who humbled himself before God and still won a decisive battle over the Midianites, stood in stark contrast to the then-prevailing view that America was back after a decade of malaise, this priest said that those who would be first must be last. Hit between the eyes with the falsity of my life, I have haltingly followed the path of humility since.

Several years later, still wondering if Jesus' indictment of lawyers was directed at me, I unburdened myself to a complete stranger leading a men's retreat. With the clarity that comes only from truth, he said: "I can think of no one who is more concerned about justice than God." Since then, I have devoted much of my life to representing the poor when the Government seeks to lock them up and throw away the key. Then there was the designer-clad tennis player who told me many years ago during the maelstrom of law school final exams that I would be a worthy opponent for his own lawyer. He introduced me to the man who has become my best friend, the older brother I never had, the selfless mentor of my career, and the guardian of the secrets of my heart as we still talk during rests on the tennis court. And finally, there was the young widow who, after losing her husband of 20 years, and at a time when I felt that I was not worthy of love, told me that she loved me.

These angels came with a message and a choice. I could hear the message and follow it, or I could ignore it. Perhaps too often I have ignored the messages of angels, but these times, I stopped to listen. These voices of my life have supported and sustained me, guided and guarded me on my walk through the valley of the shadow of death.

As you hear the stories of the angels of Christmas this year, listen to the voices of the angels of your life. You may be surprised at how close you are to God.

The Meaning of Good Friday

More than any other church holiday, Good Friday stirs up memories of its predecessors. Sure, I remember past Christmases and Easters (and maybe even a few Pentecosts), but for the most part, the secular co-option of those holidays has diminished their religious effect on me. Bunnies and Santa Clauses have supplanted the Infant Savior and the Risen Christ.

But thankfully, the popular culture can do little with Good Friday. There's something about an execution that sobers all of us, even if the networks want to broadcast them live from the gas chamber. Samuel Johnson wrote how the sight of the gallows focuses our attention completely, but even if the cross is not likely to be my ultimate fate, seeing its stark form reminds me how I have enjoyed another year in God's kingdom, still falling short of His expectations of me.

Perhaps that is why I remember Good Fridays so vividly: the elderly priest in the near-deserted church, who coughed through two-and-one-half hours of the three hours on the cross and finally said he couldn't go any further; hearing the Bishop of Atlanta beg our prayers for the latest serial murders; hearing the 33 bells toll at Trinity Church, Wall Street, in my 33rd year and wondering what I had done with my life; donating blood in a symbolic gesture; awakening from a Good Friday fast to be offered a job; sneaking worship between billable hours in New York; crying my eyes out while singing "Were You There When They Crucified My Lord," and "Sing, My Tongue, the Glorious Battle."

I don't know yet how these tiles fit into the mosaic of my life, or why I am moved more by the suffering of the victim than the innocence of an infant or the splendor of the One who rose from the dead. While I can certainly understand that without His Birth, the Crucifixion would not have happened, and without His Resurrection, the Crucifixion would be meaningless, that understanding alone does not affect me emotionally.

I know only that I have survived 40 years of near reckless disregard of the Way, the Truth and the Life, somehow embraced by the loving arms of the Son of Man who stretched them out for me on a cross. And I look forward to that Good Day when His embrace shall be eternal.

[Author's Note: This was my first essay after a gap of seven years since writing about my son on a slide. More than any other, I think it captures my belief that in faith that the only begotten Son of God died on the cross for my redemption is found the peace of God that passes all understanding.]

Afterword

The last essay I wrote for the *Anglican Advance* in Chicago doesn't fit easily into any of these categories, so it is set out below. Twelve years after the events of 9/11 which prompted this, the divine purpose behind that horrific day may be as obscure as it was when I wrote these words. But my faith remains: not in my time will God's will be done, but in His.

Finding Good in the Wake of Evil

I once worked for a state agency on the 58th floor of Two World Trade Center. In my naiveté, I thought that the job presented some physical danger, and I asked a colleague if he worried that a target of our investigations might turn on him. Matter of factly, he replied that he was as concerned about that as he was about one of the columns holding up the building collapsing. I don't know if he made it out.

Like everyone I know in these parts 800 miles removed from ground zero, I watched in stunned disbelief at the events of September 11, and the full effect has not yet kicked in. But as my former place of employment crumbled to the ground, I was reminded of the words of Solomon: "All is vanity." The same Solomon who prayed for wisdom before ascending the throne, who built the Temple to match the holy city's splendor, who ruled from the Euphrates to the Nile, could not guarantee his kingdom's security and it was divided shortly before its people were taken into captivity. Can we expect any more of our metal detectors and bomb-sniffing dogs?

Why evil exists in a world created by a loving God who sent his Son to redeem us is a question that all Christians must face. The Fall, man's disobedience, human freedom to follow the darkness can't explain why innocents are dragged into evil's snare to suffer. When evil so dominates the headlines, we cannot retort that we might as well ask why good exists. Few jetliners crash into skyscrapers out of a desire to do good.

Jesus, who wrestled with evil face to face, yet did not succumb, viewed evil as the invitation to repentance. After 18 workers were killed when an aqueduct toppled on them at Siloam, He asked whether they were more guilty than all the others in Jerusalem. Was it mere coincidence that Jesus told the young man blind from birth to wash his eyes in Siloam's pool, the spring that the workers were trying to route to Jerusalem? And was it coincidence that one of the first deaths reported was that of the New York City Fire Department's chaplain, who braved smoke and flame, falling concrete and inky darkness to minister to his flock?

Heir to a tradition which had confronted evil for two thousand years, yet never quite triumphed over it, Jesus knew well the words of the patriarch Joseph. The youngest and favorite of Jacob's 12 sons, Joseph lorded it over his older brothers. But when he tried to make peace with them, his brothers beat him up and sold him into slavery. Taken to Egypt, Joseph resisted temptation and years later became Pharaoh's confidant, to whom he predicted a terrible famine. The famine brought Jacob, his remaining sons and their families to Egypt looking for food. Revealing himself as their lost brother, Joseph welcomed his family into a land that had made provision in good harvest. Finally reconciled to his brothers after Jacob's death, Joseph fulfilled his father's last wish when he prayed that they be forgiven, saying to them: "Though you meant it for evil, God meant it for good."

About the Author

A retired lawyer now part-timing as a community activist, David G. Duggan for a number of years wrote these essays for the Christian press. He lives in Chicago, plays golf and tennis, cycles, gardens and tries to keep out of trouble. He has one son, a recently-minted MBA, living in Los Angeles.

About these essays

They were originally published in either the *Anglican Advance*, a now defunct seasonal newspaper published by the Episcopal Diocese of Chicago, or the *Living Church*, a national weekly magazine circulated to Anglicans. They are presented here in their original text, with only a handful of changes to make the temporal context clearer, or to correct typographical errors.